Divine Soul - Sacred Body
From Suicide to Sovereignty

Eliana Regina

 Be Talks Books

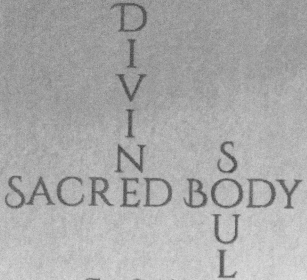

D
I
V
I
N   S
SACRED BODY   O
U
L

From Suicide
To Sovereignty

Eliana Regina

First published by Be Talks Books 2023

First edition
Editing by Alison Dale
Cover art by Renée Stotz

Disclaimer

The material in this book is not intended as a substitute for trained medical or psychological treatment or advice. The premise of this book is to unveil the mysteries and possible motives behind the act of suicide.

The author has based her arguments and conclusions on personal, professional, and spiritual experiences. The author and publisher are aware of the complexity and obscurity of this issue and assume no liability for any injuries or loss caused by the reader that may result from the reader's use of the content contained herein, and recommend sensitivity contemplating the practice described in the work.

The author would like to indicate that whilst her ideas may be controversial and/or triggering for some readers, she would also like to stress that her sole reason for speaking her truth on this particular matter is to share with the world that, although highly challenging and difficult, the road to self-healing and inner peace is not only possible but urgently needed at this time in our human journey.

Dedication

I dedicate this book to Roger's soul and all the souls who sacrificed their physical bodies for not knowing the truth about who and what they were. May this book serve in informing, inspiring, educating and empowering humans across the globe and help us solve the agonising epidemic suicide has become.

We are more powerful than we have been led to believe!

Eliana Regina

Contents

Divine Soul, Sacred Body

Foreword

By Alison Dale

I met Eliana through her connection with another author whose book I was also privileged to edit. When I read Eliana's story of trauma and transcendence, I knew I wanted to work with her. I'm a big proponent of the power of story, and have spent the last decade focused on writing, editing, and coaching others in the genre of memoir and personal narrative. Divine Soul, Sacred Body: From Suicide to Sovereignty charts Eliana's highs and lows as she faced the tragic loss of her new husband to suicide, her own similar near-demise, and the spiritual discoveries she made while uncovering her higher purpose.

During the last stretch of working on this book, a beautiful young man in my own community took his life. The ripple effect of such a loss goes beyond words and consolation, and I could feel the collective heartbreak spread through town after the news broke. It can be so challenging to understand such an agonising decision. Having stood on that slippery ledge several times in my own life, I'm familiar with the way suicidal ideation can take over one's mind, obscuring all solutions. When that happens, it can be hard to imagine ever feeling better, or that anything could possibly help. But as it's often said, suicide is a permanent solution to a temporary problem. And as Eliana says in her book, killing the body doesn't necessarily kill the pain. All of this compelled me to partner with Eliana to help her get her message out.

Eliana's husband, Roger, was a florist. And like a flower, he was both colourful and fragile – his life a brilliant bloom that burst into the world then folded in on itself. But Eliana's life purpose emerged from this tragedy. In her previous counselling career helping people struggling with suicidal ideation, Eliana created The Living Flower – a metaphorical tool for understanding oneself, one's needs, and the many aspects of the self. The book includes a conversation with a client demonstrating the tool and its ability to help shed light into dark mental places.

The whirlwind romance with Roger spun Eliana into a whole new life – one that left her forsaken at first, and unequipped to deal with the fall out. But with every one of her many moves, she righted herself and listened for guidance from her soul. She moved from place to place, each one a chrysalis for her next stage of growth and awareness. Each time, she let go of earthly attachments and possessions and just trusted. This aspect of her story inspires me greatly.

One of Eliana's main wellness practices (and one that she now teaches) is Zumba, which is all about movement. Movement is something that Eliana has mastered, and in this story, you will go with her as she lights here and there, orienting herself anew, and then releasing herself from each chrysalis like the true spiritual butterfly she came here to be.

Eliana's great respect for life permeates these pages as she celebrates the Divine Soul's desire to dance through the vehicle of the Sacred Body. Without spirit or soul animating the body, we are merely going through the motions of living. While Eliana is clear that her path may differ from others, and her words might incite controversy, she never espouses to have "the way". She just offers her life as an example of what's possible when one commits to the inner work that leads to emotional freedom. She has done the work and expressed her truth, and she invites others to do the same.

My own dedication to creativity as a path for wellness fits with Eliana's Living Flower metaphor, especially the petal reserved for self-expression. Creative expression is such a helpful way to integrate difficult and traumatic experiences back into a framework of wholeness.

Myself and a number of writing colleagues came together to create a book called *The Magic of Memoir: Inspiration for the Writing Journey.* This collection of essays covers the challenges of writing vulnerably about one's life, and Eliana has done that. It's this vulnerability that makes a bridge between people, helping them to feel less alone and overwhelmed.

It has been my honour to support the birth of this story into the world, and I fully trust it will be a help to those who read it.

Alison Dale is a writer, editor, musician, and the Founder of Soul Fire Creative.

Divine Soul, Sacred Body

Acknowledgements

First and foremost, I would like to acknowledge Spirit for guiding me through this process and giving me the insights and the courage necessary to share this message with the world.

Second, I want to thank my son who, at five years old, saved me from making a big mistake.

I would also like to acknowledge the following people who, in their own way, made this book possible:

My editor, Alison Dale, for her expertise in transforming my manuscript into a piece of art. Renée Stotz, my graphic designer, not only made the book cover and internal pages beautiful but also formatted the whole book, as a gift. Deep gratitude to you both.

I couldn't have written this book without the support of Innovate Trust, Skills & Volunteering Cymru (SVC), and Drive Wales. Thank you, Lisa French, Adrienne Earls, Sheridan Thomas and all your staff and service users with whom I've been privileged to share some Zumba fun for the past three years. I would also like to give a shout-out to Sahal, who has believed in me during this challenging process.

I want to thank Tracey Holloway for unconditionally trusting me and lending me the money I needed to buy a new laptop. Without her help, this book would not have been possible.

And finally, my beta readers, Dr Colin Young, Angela Levesque and Leanne MacDonald, for reading my manuscript and writing me a review. I would also like to thank Cal Gott for her keen eye in proofreading the final version.

PROLOGUE

Why I Am Writing This Book

Divine Soul, Sacred Body

Prologue

Divine Soul – Sacred Body: From Suicide to Sovereignty is the book I came to Earth to write. It is what my soul revealed to me as I navigated life for the past thirty-three years since losing my husband. It is my Life's Purpose.

It is a hybrid book that combines two genres:

The first two chapters are my memoir to give the reader context for the personal development aspect of the book in chapters three and four.

Chapter One will give you a glimpse of the short yet profound time I was married to Roger. He swept me off my feet in a fairy tale encounter that ended tragically when he committed suicide only fourteen months after our wedding.

Chapter Two is my 33-year personal journey – a series of rollercoasters that led me to deal with not only widowhood in a foreign country but also emotional abuse, lone parenting, depression, suicidal thoughts, financial loss, many house moves including back and forth between Brazil and Wales, and eventually a total breakdown. It presents the most critical crossroads that life presented to me: give up on life, or take the long and winding road to self-healing and personal sovereignty. My decision back in 1999 brought me to who and what I am today, writing this book.

Chapter Three, Our Divine Soul, is my attempt to share what I've discovered about my true self – a truth shared with all human souls. The personal development section of this book is interactive. Be sure to have a pen nearby as you read chapters three and four.

Chapter Four, Our Sacred Body, invites you to consider the incredible, powerful, perfect, and magical nature of the human body. My intention is to inform, inspire, educate, and empower you to also make the leap from emotional suffering to acknowledging your own sovereignty. It is in Chapter Four that I share the Living Flower metaphor and technique I have created in my work as a counsellor.

We live in highly challenging and difficult times. Confusion, distress, and despair have caused soaring suicide rates. However, in times of crisis, we are always invited to pause and find creative solutions. As a 'solutionary', it is my honour to gift you with the answers I found to resolve one of the most agonising problems of the human condition.

It is my most sincere and resounding wish that the primary message in this book will touch not only your heart but also the hearts of those you encounter, either in your personal or professional life – people who might need to heed it, too.

INTRODUCTION

Introduction

My wake-up call

I walk into my bedroom and lock the door behind me. In my left hand, I hold a bottle of powerful painkillers.

As I look out from my bedroom window, I feel the warm air of a sunny spring Sunday afternoon. I hear the hustle and bustle of the busy bumblebees sucking the nectar of rosemary flowers in my back garden.

I stare at the exuberant yellow carpet of rapeseed, and the perfect beauty and colours of springtime, but I feel numb. I glaze over the miracle of life before me and hear myself asking: *How come I am so out of sync with life and the natural beauty surrounding me?* I turn inward and 'see' a dark, chaotic, sad, and lonely inner world. The brightness of the external deepens my inner pain. I've reached the depths of my despair. I shut the curtains and I drop to my knees.

'God, or whatever force is in 'charge' here, I'm done! I can't go on like this any longer! Please pull the plug because I can't do this anymore! I have nothing left to give. PLEASE, PLEASE, just come and get me out of here! It is too damn hard! What on earth is this all about, anyway? This can't be what life is supposed to be like! Why am I so lonely? Why have I been abandoned? What have I done to have to go through this? Why do I feel like DYING??? Why do I hurt so badly? What am I doing here anyhow? I don't want to live like this. I have had enough! If I take this bunch of pills, can I slip away quietly? Will my pain end? Will it all go away? God, if you can hear me, PLEASE, ANSWER ME!'

At that precise moment, I hear my five-year-old son calling, "Mummy, Mummy...are you there?"

Immediately, I sit up from where I've been squirming on the floor like a worm, pleading with God. The sharpest, clearest question enters my mind, making me jump.

'Are you just going to give up, or are you going to dig deep so you can find all the power and all the treasures right inside of you to turn all of this around?'

More questions bombard me, slapping me awake, and jolting me out of my hypnotic 'poor me' victimhood state of mind.

'Who will take care of your son if you are gone? You have an innocent child who depends on you and you are thinking of quitting?'

Whoa! This other voice has me fully awake now. Suddenly, I'm fed up with feeling sorry for myself.

'Yes, I'm a broken-hearted, lonely woman in a strange and cold country, thousands of miles away from family and friends without any support. Yes, I'm having a hard time with depression.

Yes, I somehow became a single parent. Yes, I might have made the biggest mistake of my life, leaving Brazil to marry a stranger.'

However, I feel a knowing in me that there is something I can't quite yet see. I have the feeling that one day it will all make sense. And I will do everything I can to hold on to the belief that everything happens for a reason.

'Yes, it's eleven years since I left Brazil and my life is a mess. Roger abandoned me. I became a lone parent after having a traumatic relationship with Mark for five years. Yes, I lost my house through no fault of my own. Yes, I feel torn juggling parenting and a thriving business. I have no one to help me take care of my son. He is the only thing keeping me going. I can't be a part-time mother and a part-time entrepreneur. My business can wait. My son can't!'

I take a deep breath. I acknowledge that I've had enough of feeling like I've lost the will to live. I vow right then that I will do whatever it takes to get back to being a well-functioning human being and take good care of myself and my son. I will take responsibility for my health and well-being. I know the answer isn't in 'giving up.' Death isn't the answer. What is death anyway? How do we know what happens when the body dies? The answer can't lie in killing my body! I know I must face my pain and my suffering. I must come to terms with the traumatic events of my life and heal. My past doesn't need to determine my future.

My family blessed me with a loving upbringing that made me feel secure and supported. I felt safe and loved. I had such a sweet and happy childhood. But now I am alone, with no family around me, and no friends in a foreign land. An outsider.

'I don't belong here,' I think. 'I'm an immigrant. What am I doing here anyhow? Why did I say "Yes?" Why didn't I listen to my head instead of my heart? How did I end up in Wales alone?'

My family back in Brazil have absolutely no clue what I've been going through. How could they? They know what happened but they have no idea how badly I've been suffering. It is just me, my son, my work, and our cat Max. Wait a minute… Was I thinking of abandoning my pet too??

'No way!' I find myself saying. 'I need to turn my life around. I will do whatever it takes.'

As a mother alone, I must ensure I am well enough to be present for my child. In order to thrive as a human being, he deserves and needs the best every single child can get during these critical developmental stages. However, to be the best version of a caregiver, role model and provider for my child, I must take care of all my needs, too. I realise I have been neglecting myself, so I beg the same God or Creative Source I asked just moments ago to extinguish my light to help show me the best way to heal. To heal my body, my mind, my emotions, and my SOUL.

'Goodness, where do I start? I wonder. 'I need a path to get there. I trust the Universe will show me the way as She has always done. I have always followed the signs. Following the signs is what got me to where I am today so how can I continue trusting Her guidance?'

I feel myself neck-deep in sorrow, frustration, sadness, and grief.

Oh, the G R I E F...

Grief can literally engulf one's soul. Grief is cruel, intense, dense, and dark! Really dark. I will touch on grief again but first, I need to take you back in time to another Sunday. A dreary, damp and sinister Sunday...

Flowers to her grave

I'm rocking back and forth in the corner of my bedroom floor by the wall that separates the bedroom and the alleyway that leads to the back garden. I can hardly grasp what has just happened. It's like Spirit has left my body and left it on auto-pilot. I'm rocking back and forth to avoid the feeling of paralysis, fearing I would get stuck there. I place my hands over my ears in an attempt to silence the sounds coming from outside.

A few minutes ago, I'd heard a knock on the door and opened it, expecting to see Roger. Instead, I found two police officers. Startled, I froze.

"We received a call from your neighbour upstairs, who reported seeing a body hanging from a tree outside your flat. Is there anyone missing from your home?"

The words "Your neighbour reported seeing a body hanging from a tree" echoed in my mind for what felt like an eternity.

Now, sitting on the floor, I can't feel my body. I can only hear the dreadful, indescribable sound coming from outside – the deafening sound of a body being carried along the alleyway. I jump out of my skin when the police lady in the lounge knocks on my bedroom door, announcing I must accompany them to the hospital's morgue. It takes me a while to register what she has just asked of me. I don't respond, hoping she will leave me alone. She knocks again and, this time, opens the door gently, asking permission to come in. She offers me a cup of tea and suggests I get changed, as I need to go to the hospital to identify the body. I hear her words, but I make no attempt to acknowledge them. My soul still seems to be floating outside of my seemingly lifeless body. The lady officer helps me off the floor and sits me at the edge of the bed I had shared with Roger. I don't have any strength in me to even thank her. I can't formulate any words. In my mind, I am somewhere else. I refuse to believe what they are telling me. It must be a nightmare. I must be asleep. That's it, of course; this has to be a nightmare. I will soon wake up and see Roger sleeping next to me. I find comfort in hiding behind my wishful thoughts and keep telling myself that it's just a bad dream…just a bad dream.

Next thing I know, I am walking a long wide corridor of what seems to be a hospital. The lady officer is assisting me, as my legs no longer seem to know how to walk. We go past the chapel, and I take a moment to catch my breath. I gather any residual strength I might tap into as she escorts me towards the morgue and the worst experience of my entire life.

"Mrs. Keen," says one of the male officers, "We are going to show you the face of the person lying under that white sheet. All you need to do is tell us if you know who that person is. Let me know when you are ready. We are all here for you, Mrs. Keen."

I finally manage to nod my head, signalling I am as ready as I could ever be. He enters the room with the big glass panel, walks towards the body lying on a metal bed, and lifts the sheet. With one quick glance, I feel the life leaving my body again as I faint. When I come to, I am at the chapel being asked if I recognised the person's face.

"Yes," I respond to the officer, "Yes, that is Roger."

Earlier that dreadful night, when I returned home from a day out with my friends, I found a note from Roger saying: 'I have gone to the cemetery to take flowers to my mother's grave.' He never made it.

***

Ten years later, in my bedroom in Llandow Village once again, I stand overlooking the rapeseed field, the farms and the lambs, holding my son very tightly and telling him how much I love him and how much he means to me.

I promise myself I will take good care of my health and well-being and NEVER EVER wish my life away as I had just done a few moments earlier.

In the following pages of this book, I will take you on the 33 years journey that took me from being depressed and contemplating suicide to honouring who and what I truly am: a specialist in self-awareness and emotional literacy. I am determined to spread the message of what I believe suicide to be so that I may inform, inspire, educate, and empower open-minded individuals who are ready to embrace this truth.

Divine Soul, Sacred Body

CHAPTER ONE

My Welsh Prince Charming
Roger John
16/09/1952 – 25/11/1990

Divine Soul, Sacred Body

Chapter 1

England, March 1989

I settled into my seat for the train ride from London's Victoria Station to Dover and then across the English Channel to Belgium. My nose was buried in Albert Camus' La Peste when something made me look up. A man with long, black wavy hair wearing a light blue suit walked the aisle towards me and sat on the opposite side of the train carriage. I glanced at him through the glass window next to me. He did the same, and we noticed each other. After speaking with a couple of other passengers sitting with him, the gorgeous long-haired man got up and hurriedly left the train. So I thought. I sighed and went back to my book.

I arrived at Ostend train station, checked my luggage, and went for a walk to stretch my legs. Back at the station, I spotted a relatively spacious coffee shop to grab a cold drink and something to eat. As I walked into the noisy, crowded coffee shop, my heart started to pound. I could see nothing but the long-haired man I'd briefly glanced at earlier on the train from London.

"You are the lady from the train!" he said, approaching me as I rushed to find a table and chair to sit down before my knees gave in and I embarrassed myself.

"Small world!" I somehow muttered, still stunned by the fact that there he was again.

"Can I sit with you and get you a drink? I am delighted that the world is small enough that I can get to be in it with you! What are the odds? Just a few hours ago, we were in England, but here we are in Belgium. I have a business meeting in Brugge, and then I'm off to Paris for the weekend. Where are you heading?"

'Oh, his accent... I think I'm in love,' I thought to myself as I heard him speak. The Universe must have done a trick or two to create this encounter! I mean, really? What are the odds, indeed?

I told him I was going to Switzerland for three months, then to France and Italy for the last leg of my sabbatical from my work as a linguist. After coffee, we exchanged telephone numbers and said goodbye, as my overnight train was due to depart. I arrived in Lausanne on Saturday morning and was met by my Swiss friend Ruth. She would give me hospitality until I found a part-time job.

Ruth, her boyfriend Marcel, and I were having dinner Saturday night when the phone rang. It was Roger. I felt slightly embarrassed, having forgotten to tell Ruth I had shared her number with a stranger. I didn't think he was going to call so soon.

"Hello, lady! I can't stop thinking of our encounter. Why don't you meet me in Paris?" he suggested.

"I can't change my plans just like that. Besides, I don't even know you. How about you come to Switzerland when you can fit it into your schedule before I leave for France?"

Instead of a visit, Roger and I exchanged letters for three months, and he would frequently call me. No emails or smartphones back then. Good old-fashioned letters. I loved receiving them. Ten years older than me, Roger was a very well-travelled man. He was quite philosophical, and very romantic. "The world is your oyster, Eliana…" he once wrote. "Go find your pearl!"

I had been living in Lausanne, a French-speaking hilly city situated on the shores of Lake Geneva. Being a linguist and passionate about languages, I intended to expand my French and experience the local culture. I quickly found a job as an au pair to help me fund my stay and practice the language.

Roger knew I was off to the South of France and then to Italy to spend my last month in Europe. From Rome, I would be returning to Brazil. About a week before I was due to leave Switzerland, Roger announced in a phone call that he would visit me in Lausanne, as he could not let me go back to Brazil without seeing me again. Ecstatic, I hung up the phone with the biggest smile on my face. I couldn't wait to see him again in person.

***

Friday morning, late Spring 1989, I stood on Platform Four, waiting for the train from Belgium to arrive, bringing the long-haired, charming man.

Roger stepped off the train onto the platform holding a single red rose in his strong, solid, foxy hand with the perfectly shaped fingernails. *'Such a flawless combination of beauty,'* I thought. While somewhat short for a man, what Roger lacked in height he made up for in his presence. Roger had an exquisite aura about him and I found him deliciously attractive.

The busyness of other passengers greeting or waving goodbye to their friends and loved ones became a blur as I stood there, frozen to the spot. Elegantly dressed in a subtle blue and white striped suit, Roger walked towards me with a cheeky smile and offered me the flower. He then pulled me into a tender embrace and gave me a gentle kiss on the lips.

We spent a magically romantic week together. I had finished my work as an au pair, so I spent most of my time during those last days in Lausanne with Roger in his hotel room. We talked a lot and got to know each other's backgrounds and stories. We connected deeply and had great fun together, eating out and sightseeing, when not in each other's arms, kissing and making love. Then the day came, and it was my time to step onto a train and leave Roger and my friend Ruth to wave goodbye to me at the train station. I remember feeling slightly disoriented and emotional. Suddenly, Roger asked my friend to excuse us for a moment. He gently guided me towards the end of the platform, where it was quiet.

"I know this will sound wild, but there is only one way to say this. Eliana, I cannot let you go without you knowing my feelings. I know you have a ticket to return to your homeland from Rome in about a month. I am going to ask you a question, but I don't expect you to give me an answer straight away. I would love it if you considered it during your France and Italy trips. Then hopefully, you will make changes to your plans depending on your answer, so here it goes:

"Eliana, will you marry me?"

I don't remember a question striking me so much. As a young person, I had decided I would never get married. I thought it wasn't for me. I wanted to do a lot with my life, and getting married and raising a family wasn't part of my plans. I was on a mission to fulfil my potential and discover who I was and what I was doing here. Those two questions have guided me my whole life, and I hadn't given marriage any thought. I was 26 when Roger and I met. I was turning 27 in just a few months and was quite content with being single. I'd never been one to go on dates looking to settle down with a guy. When I was a child, I told my mother I wanted to study in a convent and become a nun. My mother – my most significant source of inspiration and a super role model – advised me against it. Knowing what I know now about organised religion, I am deeply and genuinely grateful to my mother's wisdom. However, I felt marriage wasn't for me until I met my Welsh prince. Imagine how much fun it would be to travel together for the rest of our lives! I thought. Imagine how exciting life would be with a man like Roger.

But another inner voice barged into my imaginings.

'Wait a minute, Eliana. Don't even think about doing that! You can't marry a complete stranger! You promised yourself you'd never fall into that trap.'

On the other hand, how could I not contemplate the idea of marrying my enchanting Welsh prince who came out of nowhere and swept me off my feet?

So after careful consideration, I decided to make a detour to Wales to see Roger again. I arrived at Cardiff International Airport where Roger awaited. I met his father Jack, his sister Janice, and her family, who all gave me a warm Welsh welcome. Roger had booked us a room at The Queen's Hotel in Newport. A bottle of champagne rested in an ice bucket, and rose petals were spread all over the bed. As he poured us both a glass, he gently took my left hand and kissed it softly. As our eyes locked, I felt the depth of his soul through his green eyes, mysterious and deep as the oceans. He went down on his knee and asked me again:

"Eliana, I can't bear the thought of you slipping through my fingers and missing the opportunity to spend the rest of my life with you. My beautiful lady, will you marry me?"

Overcome with emotion, I said: "Yes. *Yes*, I'll marry you, Roger, but you will have to come to Brazil, ask my parents, and get married there surrounded by my family and friends."

***

Two months later, on 16th September 1989 (Roger's 37th birthday), I walked a short but beautifully put-together open-air aisle decorated with fresh spring flowers, white ribbons tied to the rows of chairs where my family and friends gathered to honour our ceremony.

The wedding had to take place in the open air since Roger was divorced, and the Catholic Church doesn't allow divorcees to marry inside a church. And apparently, it can't be called a wedding either, so it was a "celebration." This turned out to be a blessing, as the vibe, location, trees, birds, weather, and atmosphere made the entire day magical. It couldn't have happened without the love and support of Jane, Luciano, and my Auntie Celia, who organised the whole wedding celebration in just a few weeks, taking care of the venue, the party, the music and even the bridal saloon experience. And my brother Amauri arranged for our special event to be filmed.

My father beamed with happiness and pride as he walked me to the altar near the trees. I felt like a princess as I walked along the garden path of the farmhouse my cousin Jane and Auntie Celia had rented for our special day. I wore a simple but jovial white knee-high-with-short-sleeves wedding dress, with net fabric above my cleavage, neckline and back, and matching net elbow-high sleeves attached to my middle fingers. I had pink mini roses and mini daisies on my beautifully coiffed curly brown hair, with a delicate bouquet of matching flowers. My make-up was light but defined my brown eyes more as I looked into Roger's as he took my hand.

At the altar, my cousin Devair, an ordained Catholic priest, stood waiting to perform the celebration, with my mum, godmother Celia, godfather Helio, cousin Jane and her husband Luciano standing nearby. Also present at the altar to witness and bless my union with Roger were my college friends, Sirley and her husband Bira.

As we approached the altar, my dad took a good look at me, kissed me on the forehead, and hugged Roger, who stood waiting in a blue suit, white shirt, and pink tie. I joined Roger by the altar, took a deep breath and felt ready to wed my 'prince'. The whole day felt like a fairy tale, and all family and friends present joined us in celebration and enjoyed a fabulous party afterwards. Roger's natural charisma and extroverted ways gained him a reputation as the life and soul of any party worldwide, and this was no exception. At some point during the party, Roger got hot and shed his suit jacket and pants, and spent the rest of the party in his boxers and shirt. It was just one example of his flamboyant, funny ways. My family and friends in Brazil adored him, and his broad, cheeky smile brought joy to my heart.

For our honeymoon, we travelled to Natal, a popular holiday destination and the largest city of Rio Grande do Norte, northeastern Brazil. We drove a jeep down the dunes and made love on the beach in the moonlight. We ate freshly cooked local produce at the beach restaurants and had our names written inside a little bottle filled with sand. From there, we travelled to Rio de Janeiro (a place that fascinated Roger), then took a sleeper train back to São Paulo. The whole time, I was mesmerised by this exquisite human being who made me laugh with his childlike curiosity and attempts to speak Portuguese with the locals.

Back in São Paulo, after our delicious and fabulous honeymoon, I prepared to say goodbye to Brazil and all that it represented to me. A couple of weeks later, on 4th October 1989, I arrived in Wales, Great Britain, newly married to Roger John. But since our celebration in Brazil wasn't an "official" marriage, Roger got straight into action. Before I knew it, I found myself at yet another beauty salon to prepare for our official wedding at the Registrar's Office. Once again, I was spoiled from head to toe. Whilst I sipped champagne and ate strawberries at the salon, a special delivery arrived: my wedding suit. Roger had bought me a navy-blue skirt and blazer, a silky white blouse, and a navy-blue hat. The hairdresser did my hair up in a bun, and I have never felt or looked so glamorous and elegant. Roger took care of every single detail, and I didn't have to lift one finger.

Roger loved flowers. When we married in São Paulo and again in Newport, he took care of all the flower arrangements. The most endearing was the one that he created for our first ceremony: a plate with red rose petals on a white doily where he had placed our wedding rings, which my nephew Danilo then carried to the improvised altar at the farmhouse.

On Friday, 17th November, Roger and I were officially married.

Roger was such an elegant and attractive man. His audacious taste in suits spoke volumes about his colourful personality. He loved to pair light-coloured linen suits with outrageous ties. He loved aftershave, too; his favourite was Armani. And he was such a groovy mover! At our second wedding party, he blew me away when he pulled me close to dance the Lambada, the forbidden dance, at the Irish Club in Newport.

After the party that night, and to my great surprise, he took me to our first home and carried me across the threshold. After having spent a few weeks together at his father's house, I was over the moon to have a place to call our own. Our future plan was to live in Italy, as we both loved the country and wanted to speak Italian fluently. In the meantime, we were going to settle in Newport. Roger owned a house in an elevated part of town near Beechwood Park, which he rented out during his travels. But since it was the house he'd shared with his previous wife, and where his son had been born, he rented this temporary home for us.

I was in love, and I felt like the luckiest woman alive. *'Well, I could get used to this, you know? This **married** business,'* I thought. *'What was I worried about?'* It felt like I had been blessed. Or had I?

Dudley Street, Newport, Gwent - South Wales

Home sweet home. My first home as a married woman. Again, Roger took care of all the details. Everything was so new, different, and exciting. My whole life was poles apart from anything I had ever imagined. Roger was so creative, thoughtful, and fun to be with. He was always on the go, always up to something. He was also a talented artist. Roger's pencil drawing of his son's face when he was about seven years old is still etched in my mind.

A well-spoken individual with strong opinions, Roger was also highly knowledgeable in world politics. And he was a polyglot, speaking fluent German, Spanish, Dutch, Flemish, African and Russian (plus English, of course). To say that he loved travelling is an understatement. Roger lived in many countries long enough to learn the local language and culture. He lived life to the full, and was adventurous on so many levels. He loved wearing pink, and even had a pink ski suit. One night, just for a laugh, he wore it to a local pub when we went out for a drink.

Roger sensed I was disappointed that we could not get married in a church like everybody else. Hence, as a pre-Christmas surprise, Roger booked a church ceremony and a wedding reception at the Celtic Manor Hotel on the outskirts of Newport. Roger used to provide flower arrangements to hotels and churches, and the

Celtic Manor had been one of his clients.

Despite my plan to sell my wedding dress to a bridal shop, Roger had insisted that I bring it to Wales. Now I understood. He had already planned a church wedding and kept it a secret. He invited my brother Amauri, my sister Rita, and my Swiss friend Ruth to join us on our third celebration and then spend Christmas with us.

One evening before dinner, I was in the shower when I heard him come in. He opened the shower curtain and gazed at me from head to toe with a cheeky, mischievous look on his face. Then he jumped into the shower, fully dressed, reached into his pocket, took out a beautiful emerald engagement ring, and said: "I have been looking for a special ring to fit the finger of a special lady. I know I have asked you this question before, but I'll ask you again, just to make sure. Eliana, my beautiful lady, will you be my wife?"

Roger placed the ring on my left finger, took his clothes off, and we made love under the shower.

An incorrigible romantic, Roger was always surprising me with flowers and gifts. One night, I woke up around 4 a.m. to the smell of cooking. Roger was not beside me in bed, so I got up to investigate. I found him in the kitchen, cooking a steak and mushroom dinner with French mustard and sautéed potatoes. He was naked except for an apron and a cook's hat. When he saw me coming, he said: "Just in time. Pour yourself a glass of wine whilst I'm finishing off the cooking, and I'll be dishing us the best steak you have ever eaten!"

"Roger, it's 4 o'clock in the morning!"

"Best time to start your day! And what's better than French cuisine and red wine as *petit déjeuner*?"

Roger was one of those people who didn't need much sleep. He'd go to bed late and get up before dawn. He'd sleep less than four hours and be ready for the day ahead, bright and early.

After eating our steak dinner for breakfast that morning, we made passionate love in the dining room. Roger was a gentle, thoughtful lover. He didn't have a high sex drive, which suited me perfectly since I was never that much interested in sex either. But when we made love, it was pure magic.

After lovemaking and a shower, he invited me to go out to work with him that day. At that time, as well as his flower arranging business, Roger ran a flower and plant stall at various markets, so he was always gone early to buy fresh flowers when they arrived at the docks. On that fun and memorable morning, we sold lots of flowers and I got to see him in action, charming his customers.

A few days later, my brother and sister arrived at Cardiff International Airport in time for our church wedding on 19th December, 1989. My friend Ruth also attended the wedding. It was quite a big do at the Celtic Manor Resort and yet another memorable day. The Bellamies (my British family from Exeter, where I studied before meeting Roger) came, as well as Lynn and Michael Sullivan, the family I worked for as an au pair after my studies in Exeter, looking after their children, Nicola and Christopher. I was delighted to see them all again.

My brother and sister spent Christmas with us, and then the four of us travelled to Amsterdam in the red Volkswagen Polo Roger had bought me for Christmas. So much happened in such a short time. From Amsterdam, my brother and sister caught a train to Switzerland to spend the New Year with Ruth whilst Roger and I checked into a nudist spa for a retreat. *Being married to Roger is never going to be boring*, I thought many times, as he was always coming up with outrageous ideas!

On our return to Wales, Roger enrolled me at the local college to learn German and offered to help me write a curriculum vitae, so I could pursue my career as a linguist. Everything was going so well, and I was thrilled until Roger announced we were moving house.

Clevedon Road, Newport (January to April 1990)

I wasn't keen on the idea of living in the house where Roger lived with his ex-wife, but I went along with it. I realised I had been dependent on Roger for too long, and that was making me feel uncomfortable. I had always been independent, so I started thinking of getting a casual job until I decided how to resume my career as a translator, interpreter and language teacher.

Only a few months ago, I'd been telling myself I was wrong to fear falling in love and that I could open my heart and fully embrace a relationship in a way I never thought possible. I'd wanted to become a nun, remember? Meeting Roger changed everything.

But when we moved into Clevedon Road, Roger's behaviour changed. He stopped paying attention to me. In fact, we hardly saw each other, as he was rarely home. But what concerned me most was his drinking, now a daily habit.

'What is happening?' I wondered. *'What has happened to my fairy tale? Where has my gorgeous, awe-inspiring gentle prince gone? I don't understand! Who is this drunk, snoring man sleeping next to me?'*

When Roger and I had spent our first week-long date in Lausanne, we were out for lunch one day, and we got talking about our families. I remember Roger broke down in tears when he told me his mother had died suddenly of a heart attack five years before. As he'd been travelling and living abroad for several years after his divorce, he'd been out of the country at the time. Though I had no idea what was happening within him, I sensed that something was unresolved. But back then, I had no understanding of depression, and unbeknownst to me, Roger was suffering from it.

I hated living in that house, haunted as it was by memories of his previous life. People came and went all the time. Roger told me they were his business acquaintances. I felt invisible, and Roger ignored me. He was out all the time and frequently came home drunk.

Things changed dramatically one day when Roger received a letter from the Council Tax. I don't recall the details, but I do recall his actions. It must have been around March 1990, and we had been married for six months. Jack came over and told me Roger had been arrested. Apparently, he'd gone to the Civic Offices with an unloaded bazooka and threatened the staff at the reception because he'd received a bill which he thought was a mistake.

'Well, how would that have turned out?' I wondered. *'What was he thinking? And where on earth did he get a bazooka from?'*

Roger was released on bail and was due to appear in court. One night, still around March 1990, Roger didn't come home. I was awakened by a phone call from Gwent Police in the middle of the night, announcing Roger had been arrested for drunk driving. He had taken my car that night, and I didn't know.

Suffice it to say that my whole world came crashing down. I felt lost and bewildered, and wondered if I had made a terrible mistake. I had no one to talk to, and I certainly didn't want to worry my family, as they could do nothing. They thought I was living life like a princess when in fact, I was scared and lonely. I started having serious headaches. They turned out to be migraines. I had never suffered from migraines before and hardly ever experienced headaches. Confused and concerned, I had no idea what would happen next.

One day, a friend of Roger's came by. Her name was Zoe. Zoe de Lucca. She knocked on the door and wanted to speak to Roger, who was out. Roger was always out. Zoe was pregnant and seemed somewhat anxious to speak with him. As I invited her in and offered her a cup of tea, I broke down in tears. I had not spoken to anyone for a while and didn't know what to do about what I was going through. It seemed to me that I fell in love with one man but got married to another. I was beginning to resent Roger and felt forsaken. I resented him being out every night. I resented leaving my dreams of running a language school in Brazil. I missed my family, friends, and my home country. I told

Zoe what was going on.

Next thing I know, she said: "Right! You're coming with me. Where are your personal things, clothes, etc?"

Zoe threw a bed sheet across the bed and filled it with all my belongings. I had never seen someone act so quickly on a split-second decision. "We don't have time to waste. Come on, let's go! Roger will have me to answer to. How dare he do this to you? Don't worry, Eliana. I have known Roger long enough to know when he oversteps the mark and needs a wake-up call."

Cromwell Road, Newport (April to August 1990)

So with that, I left Roger and moved in with Zoe, her 2-year-old son, her dogs, and an also-pregnant cat. I planned to return to Brazil and then divorce Roger. The problem was that I didn't have access to my money. Since my family and friends couldn't give us physical gifts for our wedding, they'd all given us money to start our lives in Wales, but Roger said he'd invested it in his flower business.

I got myself a job as a shop assistant at River Island, a High Street clothes shop, which allowed me to practice my English language skills. Unfortunately, Roger got angry and started harassing me at my place of work and at Zoe's house. I felt so confused. I had never experienced anything like that, and I felt intimidated and anxious. He used to hang around Zoe's house and knock on the door, demanding I return home with him.

Zoe suggested I needed to report him and encouraged me to get an injunction against him. I had never heard of this terminology and didn't quite understand its implications. But I went along with it, as I didn't have anyone else to help me and didn't know what to do in a strange country. I got an injunction against Roger, my own husband, which meant he was not supposed to come anywhere near me. I found myself another job, as a secretary, thinking he wouldn't find out.

A couple of months passed. The World Cup in Italy was starting in early June, and I knew Roger was going to watch it. Originally, we were supposed to go together. We had planned to explore Italy after the football match, so we could start creating the possibility of living there. Roger somehow found out the location of my new place of work, as one day, the postman came with a postcard he'd sent to me from Italy. A letter followed, and then another one. Roger was asking me to forgive him. He said we needed to talk to work things out. I was touched. My Prince Charming was back, and I fell for him again.

When the World Cup was over and he returned to Newport, we started meeting at the park, where I felt safe. Roger said he was really sorry for what he had put me through and assured me he would never do anything to upset me ever again. He would stop drinking and be the husband and life partner he had promised to be, in accordance with our wedding vows. So, I believed him, gave our marriage another chance, and suggested we move from Newport, as I didn't like it there.

Richmond Road, Cardiff (August 1990 to March 1991)

In August, just after my 28th birthday, Roger and I left Newport and moved to Cardiff, the capital city of Wales. We rented a lovely ground-floor flat with a back garden, near the city centre. I was super excited to start over, and on 16th September, on our first wedding anniversary (also Roger's 38th birthday), he took me out for dinner at TGI Fridays on Newport Road.

Roger had given up drinking alcohol but also seemed to have given up laughing, joking, dancing and even sex. I was out working, and Roger stayed at home. He would cook our evening meals, and we'd sit together, but he seemed absent and not in the mood to talk. We had no TV, and I did my best, based on whatever social skills I had at the time, to hold space for him and ask him to share what was going on for him, but to no avail. Roger didn't want to talk. After insisting that he tell me what was going on and if there was anything I could do, he revealed that he'd been required to see a psychiatrist after the bazooka incident. He didn't want to tell me any details about these sessions, and I respected that. There was something else he didn't tell me which became evident a couple of months later.

Roger and I would usually walk to Tesco on Albany Road for our weekly shopping. (He'd crashed the car he had given me, and we no longer had our own transport.) Roger wouldn't go out much anymore and was no longer working. He'd go on the train to Newport once a week to see his father, Jack, but apart from that, Roger spent his time at the flat. I never knew how he was spending his time other than keeping the flat clean and tidy and cooking our evening meal. I was still working in Newport as a secretary in a small office, which I quite liked.

I felt very isolated, so I looked at getting a phone line as we didn't have mobile phones back then. I needed to be able to talk to my family every now and then and call Roger during the day from work to check on him. I thought it would be good for Jack to speak to Roger more often, as well. Then I remembered my university friend, Eliane Bandeira, who also married a British man and immigrated to the UK as well. I looked up her number and called to invite them over for a visit. It so happened that it was Eliane's birthday on Sunday, 25th November, so it was the perfect opportunity to get together. Eliane and her husband, Chris, would drive to Cardiff from their home in Bournemouth on the south coast of England.

My friends arrived on Friday. Roger cooked us a lovely meal, and then on Saturday, we took them on a bit of a tour of Cardiff. Roger seemed his old cheerful self and was a perfect host. We all went out for pizza in the evening and shared some wine. After abstaining for the past few months, Roger also enjoyed a couple of glasses.

Chris was into caves and wanted to take a trip to visit The Big Pit National Coal Museum on Sunday. It was Eliane's birthday, and we planned to have lunch after the museum, but Roger decided not to go. He reminded me it was also the anniversary of his mother's death, and he had plans to go to the cemetery in Newport with Jack, which I totally understood. I kissed him goodbye, closed the door, and headed out with my friends.

That was the last time I saw Roger alive.

When we returned later that dreadful, misty, dark and sombre November evening, I found a note from Roger saying: 'Have gone to take flowers to my mother. Roger xxx.' The note was written in small, almost illegible letters. I cooked a quick pasta dish for my friends and me before they set off back to Bournemouth and set some aside for Roger.

It was getting late. My friends had already left so I drew a hot bath, then waited a little longer for Roger. I had work in the morning, so I decided to go to bed and figured he had stayed in Newport with Jack. *'He could have called or added to his note',* I thought as I went to bed. I decided it was best not to call Jack to check on Roger, as I felt they needed privacy. Plus, I didn't quite know what to say as I knew how upset he would get when talking about his mother. I remembered how drunk he got the year before, and I was sure he and Jack appreciated having the day together.

Except, he never got to Jack's.

He never made it to the cemetery, either.

In fact, he never left the grounds of our flat…

I had fallen asleep when a loud knock on the door awakened me. I jumped out of bed, thinking Roger must have lost or forgotten his key and was finally home. To my shock, however, it was two police officers who came to inquire if someone was missing from my home – the same two officers who carried Roger's dead body along the alleyway while I sat on my bedroom floor with my hands over my ears…

My darling Roger,

Our time together was short but profound. You came waltzing into my life, took me by the hand and led me to an unfamiliar dance floor. You introduced me to Gypsy Kings, and we danced the Lambada. And then poof… just as you arrived, unannounced, you left…

I have battled with the idea of one day sharing our story with the

32

world and revisiting all the memories I'd buried deep inside me. The idea took the shape of an important message and grew more significant than the resistance I was struggling with and more meaningful than my personal life.

I had no skill set even to comprehend what had happened. After a while, I put it away in my subconscious mind and pretended it had never happened. We humans do that when everything we are going through is too overpowering to process. We seem to have learned, or even been encouraged to suppress, deny, numb out, and then get depressed. And if we don't recognise what's happening and don't ask for or look for help, we might end up doing what you did.

Your soul and the essence of what I experienced in the short time we were married are etched in my soul. I, too, suppressed, denied, and numbed out. There were many cycles of depression I battled through. I, too, had thoughts of ending my life. Believe me, I get it. I have been there! Luckily, I realised it in time and had the discernment to know that suicide wasn't the answer. I was also lucky that my child called out to me. So here I am, 33 years later, with over 20 years of inner work, personal development, and a career in Counselling to "innerstand" what suicide is really about. I somehow knew that killing myself would never truly solve anything.

I am so sorry for the pain you were in. I am sorry for your suffering. I'm sorry you suddenly lost your mother, but it wasn't your fault! And I'm sorry you didn't know how to ask for help.

*We are **Divine Souls in a sacred human body having a physical experience.** Our experiences cause us to feel the emotions they evoke. I believe the lack of self-awareness and lack of emotional literacy is what really killed you. I cannot accept that a human being who knows* *they are a fractal of the creative source that sparked the Universe into being would extinguish their creative light. It doesn't make sense!*

The suicide rate keeps rising worldwide, including children and young people, and I feel it is time for this message to be shared.

*We have to wonder why we are killing ourselves **and** each other. We have to ask why this seems to have become acceptable and so mainstream. We have to stop this. We have to learn how to heal ourselves. How to heal our wounds, innerstand who and what we are and acknowledge our **Sovereignty**.*

I sincerely wish that Divine Soul – Sacred Body will reach the hands and hearts of millions of open-minded individuals who will heed the message in this book to empower themselves so that they can empower others – especially those in the field of Counselling, Psychotherapy, Psychology and Social Sciences professionals.

As for you, my darling Roger, I am sorry I didn't know then what I know now. I'm sorry I haven't been able to help and empower you. I promise you I will not allow your sacrifice to go in vain. It comforts my heart to imagine that you found your way to your mother's arms and felt cradled by her love and that together, you are both safely home with our Maker.

I created The Living Flower as a metaphor in your honour to inform, inspire, educate, and empower those ready to embrace the truth I have come to know. I sincerely trust our story together will touch the hearts of many and save the lives of thousands.

Rest in peace, my darling.

Eliana, your 'lady.'

CHAPTER TWO

Two Countries, Three Phases, Thirty-One
House Moves, Thirty-Three Years
and Too Many Trips to Count!

From Auto-Pilot to Total Breakdown

1990–2001

Chapter 2

Alone at Richmond Road

After having to be the one to recognise Roger's dead body at the hospital's morgue came the distressing, traumatic inquest process. The cause of death registered on Roger's death certificate stated:

'Hanging: Killed himself whilst suffering the illness of depression.'

By then, my sister Rita had flown over to support me and help me move back to Brazil after the funeral. My friends Eliane and Ruth also came.

In December 1990, Roger was buried beside his mother's grave at St. Woolos Cemetery in Newport. The whole thing is a blur, to be frank. Confusion, disbelief, and sadness had taken hold of me.

After the funeral, I packed my bags and booked my ticket home with my sister. But two days before our flight, I received a letter from what was then The Polytechnic of Wales. Remember when Roger helped me write my curriculum vitae? I didn't realise that he'd mailed some to agencies, one of them being the Welsh Development Agency. They passed on my details to the Polytechnic, who invited me to teach a Portuguese language intensive to Law undergraduate students. The eight-week position started in January 1991, and paid a handsome fee of £21 an hour, four hours per day, Monday to Friday.

This attractive offer conflicted with my plan to return to Brazil and pick up where I had left off. My career in languages waited for me there. However, having the experience of teaching Portuguese in Wales would undoubtedly look pretty damn good on my C.V., so I decided to accept the position. After spending Christmas with my family, I would return to Wales for a couple of months.

Back at Richmond Road, alone and in denial, I did my best to keep it together and focus on the course I was about to deliver. But after a couple of months of struggling to stay at the flat, I knew I had to move.

In contrast with having lived in the same house with my parents and siblings for over twenty years, this would be my sixth time moving house in less than two years, including the massive transition from Brazil to Wales. I didn't realize that all this upheaval might actually be serving my higher purpose, and that each place would serve as a chrysalis for the series of transformations that lay ahead. With every subsequent move, my role as a spiritual butterfly emerged.

Short Spell at Spencer Street

I found a temporary room in a shared house for rent on Spencer Street in Cardiff, near where I'd lived with Roger. I shared a two-bedroom house with a French student with whom I got on quite well. The plan was to deliver the Portuguese course and return to Brazil to pursue my dream of running a language school.

I fell in love with teaching my native language and creating unique content. The intensive course turned into an extensive one, and the head of Modern Foreign Languages asked if I would run the course until June, when the students would be going to Portugal. Since I was loving the work, without much thought I said: "Of course! Would love to."

When I got home that day, I realised that in order to meet my monthly expenses, I would need another job to complement my teaching. Suddenly, opportunities started to appear out of nowhere. Soon I had a part-time job as a receptionist at a hotel, an evening job selling newspapers subscriptions, and a Saturday job at a photography studio. At one point, I was working every single day of the week. This served a physical and psychological purpose: I had to make my body and mind so tired that I could sleep. Since I had no clue how to deal with Roger's suicide, I pretended it never happened. Work had become my coping mechanism. I was on auto-pilot mode.

One day, I received a phone call from the Welsh Development Agency. They had a small business based in Treforest Industrial Estate, near the Polytechnic, that needed a Portuguese/English translator and interpreter to help them source business in Portugal. The company was a loudspeaker manufacturer with the original idea of encasing speakers in a ceramic urn-like ornament. I sourced a company in Oporto, Portugal, to produce the ceramic urns. Peter Wilson, the loudspeaker engineer with his team, would then assemble the loudspeakers in our workshop.

After several months of freelancing with the company, the two partners offered me a permanent position running the office. Eventually, I became the Import & Export Director and Company Secretary in charge of running the office and the financial affairs of the business on a full-time basis.

And that's where I met Mark.

Nine months had passed by since that tragic Sunday in November. Roger's birthday – and our wedding anniversary date – was approaching. Then I received news that Jack was in the hospital. A few days later, he died – I believe of a broken heart. Roger meant the world to him, and even though he had a daughter and grandchildren, I imagine Jack's loss was too intense to think beyond it.

Grief can do that to you. It can throw you into a sea of deep sorrow, seize your mind, tear your heart into little pieces, and claim your soul if you let it. That's how powerful emotions can be if not felt, processed, and healed (a conversation for another book entirely).

Everything was still very raw, and Jack's death reminded me of it all so I went home again for Christmas with the family. I had an invitation to join Delphine, my French roommate, to spend New Year's in New York City. So, from Brazil, I flew to the Big Apple for the first time. We welcomed 1992 at Time Square, where I told my friend I had started the proceedings to buy my own house and that I would be leaving Spencer Street.

Resilience at Rowan's Lane

Just before my 30th birthday in August 1992, I moved into a brand-new house on Rowan's Lane near Bridgend. I'd watched the two-bedroom terrace house being built from the ground up, and it came complete with carpets, curtains, and a built-in oven and hob. It had a small piece of land for a garden and a private drive to park the car I still needed to get. I didn't have a single piece of furniture either, so I bought a sofa bed and a fridge. When I moved in, I suddenly asked myself:

'What has just happened? How on Earth am I going to return to Brazil now?'

Then there was Mark, a printer who created promotional material for Brinkman, including my own business cards. Drawn to each other, we began dating, and when I moved into Rowan's Lane, things started getting serious. Mark enchanted me with the idea of raising a family and growing old together. On the 4th October 1993, exactly four years after I arrived in Wales married to Roger, Mark moved in.

Since we had been thinking of starting a family, it made sense for us to live together. There had been no talk about getting married, but the important thing was to be together and have a healthy, happy relationship.

Late one November, a Saturday morning as I recall, after Mark had gone to the office, I sat at the edge of my bed with my eyes closed, counting to sixty for the third time. I needed three minutes before I checked the result. With my left hand over my heart, and a pregnancy test in my right hand, I finished the last count.

'Fifty-nine, sixty! Okay, whatever the result, I accept, knowing that everything happens for a reason and in Divine timing.' I lowered my left hand to touch my stomach and examine the test results. "Oh, my goodness," I exclaimed. "It's positive! It's positive! I am going to be a mother! I am going to have a baby!!!" Overwhelmed, I burst into tears of joy.

'I can't tell Mark over the phone,' I thought. *'I'm going to have to wait for him to come home. Oh, my goodness, he's going to leap with joy.'*

Having a child was his idea to begin with, and it took some persuasion on his part. Bringing a child into this world full of challenges and traumas was a scary thought to me, and needed careful consideration from both parties. It wasn't until Mark started talking about it that I realised my biological clock was ticking. If I wanted to do this, I'd have to jump in and embrace it right away. I didn't want to be a geriatric mother, and 31 was already pushing it! But the results were positive, and positively thrilling. I felt so blessed!

Mark came home mid-afternoon after finishing work at lunchtime. As usual, he had stopped at the local pub for a drink. I was still smiling and wrapped in a bubble of joy. As he came through the door, I couldn't control my excitement.

"Come and sit down a minute, Mark. I have something to tell you." Before he could say anything, the words "I AM PREGNANT" burst out of my mouth as if by themselves. "We are going to have a baby!"

"Did you do the test on your own?" he shouted. "Why didn't you wait for me? You should have waited for me!"

My bubble burst, and my smile turned into a frown. Mark's words and tone of voice cut into my joy like a sharp knife, momentarily killing it. I didn't know how to respond but heard myself saying: "I'm so sorry, Mark. I just felt it was such an intimate thing to do. I'm really, really sorry. I didn't realise you wanted to be there whilst I peed on a stick! What's more important than the actual news of us being pregnant? Please, let's celebrate this moment, yeah?"

"Of course, I'm sorry too. I didn't mean to shout or scare you. That's amazing, Eliana. Well done, you! Such great news, Babe. Come here." Mark hugged me and placed his hand over my belly.

The following month Mark and I went to Brazil for Christmas so he could meet my family. We stayed at Hotel Duas Marias near Campinas, São Paulo estate, about 60 miles from the capital city bearing the same name (where my brother Amauri lives). We all had a great time together, then went to Cambuquira, in the state of Minas Gerais, to visit my college friends Sirlei and Bira and their two boys, Raoni and Cauê.

Back in Wales, in January 1994, only about eight weeks into my pregnancy, Mark's behaviour started to change. All of a sudden, my every move had to be accounted for. I felt interrogated all the time and I didn't understand what was happening.

My work at Brinkman's, the loudspeaker manufacturers, had ended when the company failed, but I found a job with a small export company in Bridgend, close to my home. Unfortunately, my boss suspected I was pregnant and sacked me. Devastated, as I really liked the job, I also felt like I'd been wrongfully dismissed. But Mark didn't mind and said it would be best for me to stay home anyway. So, I did.

I loved being pregnant and I felt fantastic! I enjoyed every developmental phase and kept a baby diary, where I kept all my pregnancy related appointments, and journalled about my feelings and the milestones. I felt blessed and grateful that Mark and I had the long conversations before we both agreed to consciously conceive a child. This is a very important decision and one I would encourage all couples to make well before a pregnancy changes their lives, which it most certainly will. A human conception is precious, as human life is sacred. To carry the Divine Soul of another human life inside us is simply miraculous. Humanity could very well transform naturally if all pregnancies were planned and carefully discussed.

My mother flew over before the baby was due, and in August 1994, our son was born. It was a long and traumatic delivery with complications afterwards. Mark took me and the baby home, but after a few days, I started hemorrhaging and was rushed into the hospital for an emergency dilation and curettage (D&C). The doctor had left bits of placenta behind after butchering me and leaving scars on my son's temples due to the barbaric forceps method.

My mother had already gone back to Brazil for her work commitments, and I felt very alone with no one to support me. Although I was confident that Mark loved me and our baby, he didn't help me care for our son. I was still recovering from the operation and the traumatic birth, and our relationship started to suffer. I felt exhausted and confused. By Christmas 1994, I had fallen into depression – the first in a long cycle that lasted many years, each time getting deeper and darker.

Overwhelmed, alone and not knowing what to do, I went to see a doctor, who prescribed anti-depressants. Since I was breastfeeding, I refused to take any medication. I chose to focus on caring for my baby and myself the best way I could. When my son was nine months old, I took him to Brazil for the first time to meet his family across the Atlantic.

When he turned a year old, I turned a corner too, and started enjoying every moment of motherhood, especially the first summer with my baby. I loved taking him out to parks and spending time in our back garden playing together, sitting in the warm sun.

I had updated my curriculum vitae to work as a translator from home. In October 1995, I started teaching Portuguese as a target language at Cardiff University's Lifelong Learning Centre. It was an evening course, which meant Mark could stay home with our son whilst I slowly returned to work. Even though Mark supported us the best way he could, his business wasn't doing well, and finances were tight. As a couple, we weren't doing well either, so I started reading books on relationships and did my best to keep things together.

In the summer of 1996, I took my son to Brazil again, where he spent his second birthday. It so happens that he was born on my Godmother and nephew's birthday, so it was a triple celebration that year.

A break from the relationship and quality time with my family revived me. I returned to Wales feeling fresh and optimistic. However, things at home hadn't improved. I felt suffocated and unable to be myself. Mark became more and more demanding and verbally abusive.

In 1997, when our son turned three and started nursery school, I announced that I would be returning to college in September. I had enrolled at Bridgend College to do a psychology course. I desperately wanted to understand what was happening in my relationship, and whilst in college, I started seeing a counsellor. That year, I also came across NLP (Neuro-linguistic Programming) and took a diploma course on the subject.

Unfortunately, the verbal and emotional abuse at home got worse, and things were starting to get out of hand. One evening, after reading my son a few stories and settling him into bed, I plunged onto the sofa, exhausted. Mark was watching *Robot Wars* on BBC Two, a programme I despised. He got up to get something to eat from the kitchen. In the meantime, I flicked through the channels to see what else was on. Mark came back and saw that the T.V. was switched to another channel. In a rage, he threw the plate of food at the wall.

"What did you change the channel for?" he shouted.

"I was just looking through whilst you were in the kitchen. Come on, calm down. There's no need to shout at me like that."

"Well, I was watching Robot Wars, so switch it over right now and go and clean up that mess."

"Are you for real?" I answered. "You made the mess; you clean it up. I'm off to bed. Good night!"

My heart pounding with fear and dread, I retreated to my bedroom. I didn't want my son to be raised under these circumstances, and the verbal abuse was escalating into something more serious. I prayed for an amicable solution.

A few days later, I spotted a leaflet for a start-up grant and course on starting your own business – something I'd been wanting to do. Our son would be in primary school the following year, so I signed up for the course. Later that day, as I started telling Mark of my plans, he lost his temper and raised his hand to slap me. I put my hand up and looked straight into his eyes.

"Don't you dare ever, ever touch me! I think we have come as far as we can, Mark. It seems to me the more I do to please and understand you, the more you demand and the less you appreciate me."

Though frightened about his reaction, I told Mark to leave.

Our separation was ugly and traumatic, and due to the threat of violence, it involved the local police.

About a year later, in October 1998, I managed to launch my language business, ERN Global Links. I offered interpreting services mainly to the South Wales Constabulary, solicitors' firms, and the courts. With my translation and teaching work going well, in February 1999, I was able to take my son to Brazil for another visit. I desperately needed to see my family and recharge, and these visits were an antidote to depression.

Whilst in Brazil, I invited my nephew Danilo, who had just finished his secondary education, to come to Wales to study English and help me look after my son while my business took off. I was not too fond of leaving my son with childminders. Having Danilo around and speaking Portuguese at home meant my son was brought up bilingually, an asset he would have for life.

Engulfed by despair at East View

After living at Rowan's Lane for seven years, in April 1999, I decided to move to a different location. I needed a bigger place, as my cousin's daughter, Wanessa, came over to study English, too. I rented my house to a woman who was also a single parent. We moved into a lovely detached house in a quaint, peaceful village, with a big garden overlooking expansive farm fields, and where my son could play on the street with other kids.

After settling into our spacious new home for a few months, my nephew and my cousin's daughter finished their courses and returned to Brazil, as their student visas were running out. Around the same time, my tenant stopped paying the rent. I couldn't evict her because she had a child and the 'law' on her side. On top of feeling overstretched from running a business and being a single parent, I wasn't coping very well with the tenant issue. I couldn't afford to pay the mortgage on top of the rent, all the bills, and all the other living costs, so after several months in arrears, the bank repossessed the house. I fell into a deeper depression and started self-medicating with alcohol in an attempt to numb my pain, sorrow, confusion, and loneliness.

That warm Sunday afternoon when I stood in my bedroom

overlooking the rapeseed fields, pills in hand and ready to end my life, is the day I hit rock bottom. My son's voice calling for me pulled me back to my life and my sense of purpose. I took him into my lap and cuddled him then. In my mind and heart, I silently asked him to forgive me for contemplating the dreadful thought of leaving him behind like that.

'Please forgive me, son. I promise I will take good care of myself so I can take good care of you.'

I made an appointment with my GP (General Practitioner). The following day, I sat in the doctor's office on a chair across from his desk. I started talking and suddenly burst into tears. As I sobbed my heart out, the phone rang. And he answered it! When he put the phone down, he got out his prescription book, wrote me a prescription for Prozac, and told me to see him again if the symptoms persisted.

'Excuse me?' I thought to myself as he handed me the prescription. *'Did that actually happen??'*

I left his office and have not consulted with a doctor ever since! I have never been keen on conventional treatment and pharmaceutical medication anyway, so I decided to trust my intuition and look for alternative ways to heal my depression and its effect on my life. My son needed me. I needed me!

I started listening to my inner guidance. I closed my business so I could focus on being a full-time mother, and embarked on my healing journey. I began researching alternative treatments for depression, and synchronicities started to happen. That's when I came across kinesiology, Reiki, mantras, meditation, and self-help books. I started learning about my spiritual anatomy and dedicated time and effort into my spirituality. I learned that equal to our physical anatomy with the organs, limbs and all the body parts, humans have a metaphysical side.

The more I learned about this metaphysical side of my being, the more curious and fascinated I became. I realised how much I had neglected myself, not to mention the alcohol I abused to avoid dealing with the underlying issues causing my depression. I had been self-medicating. Can you relate? So easily done as alcohol is heavily advertised and we're encouraged to consume it.

Once I committed to doing the inner work necessary, I realised there were layers of issues I needed to peel off my emotional body. I learned in one of the books I read that our 'issues are in our tissues,' but they don't belong there! It seems to me we humans have become conditioned to keep our traumas deep in our subconscious minds. We are good at ignoring all the early signs our bodies send in their efforts to get our attention. But traumas do not belong in the body!

Inner work is a challenging and never-ending journey, but once I embarked on it, I never looked back. My health and well-being depend on how I treat all aspects of my being: my body, mind, soul, and emotions. As a responsible adult, it is up to me to look after myself and nourish all these aspects of life as a human being.

I started by taking a good look at everything I had gone through for the past eleven years since I left Brazil. I desperately wanted to release the suffering from my energetic field so that I could transform and grow. Once I felt steadier and more in control, I followed my inner guidance, trusting it unconditionally.

I sensed that another physical move would assist in the healing process. A new start was in alignment with the millennium, so in January 2001, we moved to another village nearby.

April Cottage Part 1: A stepping stone

Despite all my efforts, I was still in a bad place. Feeling forsaken and abandoned in the wilderness of loneliness, I turned back to alcohol. Once my son was tucked in bed, a nightly bottle of wine became my faithful companion.

Mark had taken me to court when we split up to prevent me from making any major decision that affected our child. At the time, I took it personally, feeling he was still controlling my life. But I eventually came to respect him for taking that route. I was in a real mess and needed some time out. I begged Mark to authorise me to go to Brazil with our son for six months, but he only allowed me to go for three. I took it, and in June, after meeting my new landlord, Arthur Benbow, who had been cycling the world after his wife's death, my son and I went home to spend time with family and friends.

A couple of weeks following our return to Wales, 11th September happened, and I freaked out. The trip to Brazil had soothed my soul, but I knew there was still much inner work to do, and the loneliness threw me back into the wilderness.

After our separation, Mark moved to London, where he was born and where his father still lived. He would pick up our son, taking my boy to London for half-terms and holidays using public transport. While they were away, I struggled with the overwhelming feeling that the over-and-underground trains in London weren't safe.

My restless soul nudged me to take some action. I went to see a solicitor and told her my story. I needed to return to Brazil and take my son to live there with me. I wasn't coping, and my deepening depression scared me. The solicitor gave me a long list of things I needed to comply with before applying to the courts and being granted permission to take my son out of the country for good. I was in no state to meet these requirements.

Another nudge from my soul made me reach out to the Brazilian Consulate in London for guidance. Thankfully, in those days, we could ring and speak to a human being. I was relieved when the kind and empathic civil servant, after carefully listening to me, said:

"Pack your bags and go. Take your son and fight for your rights through the Brazilian Courts, where your family will help and support you."

I had no one I could trust except my Italian friend, Francesca Jackson, who helped me with spiritual guidance and a car boot sale to raise the necessary funds I needed. I sold my car and everything else I could sell and gave the rest to charities.

On 21st October 2001, I fled Wales with my son and our cat, Max.

From Breakdown to Breakthrough

2001-2012

Goodbye Wales, I'm going home!

We departed from Cardiff International Airport in time to surprise my mother on her 70th birthday the following day. On our way to the airport, I dropped three letters in the letter box. One to my solicitor, one to my son's school, and one to the local authorities, informing them of my decision to leave. I said that I would deal with the consequences of my actions in Brazil, where I would have the necessary emotional support.

Leaving Wales without Mark's consent was a bold move. To this day, I have no idea where I got the strength to pull that off. I knew deep down I was doing the right thing – both for my well-being as well as my 7-year-old son's best interest. It was a massive act of trust on both sides. I explained to him that he couldn't tell anyone; otherwise, we would risk being unable to go. He didn't need much convincing, since the three months he had spent there earlier in the year, climbing trees, fishing in the lakes, playing with cousins and being adored by grandparents, aunties and uncles gave him a taste of a completely different lifestyle – one that he absolutely loved.

Safe and Sound in São Paulo

My family had no idea what was happening but welcomed my son and me with open arms. My mother was delighted to have me home again, this time not just on an escape from feeling depressed. I felt nurtured, safe, heard and held on many levels by different people, simply by their physical presence in my life again. Initially, I spent a couple of months with my family in São Paulo. There I waited to hear from my solicitors in Wales about Mark's response. I also needed to figure out what I would do and where I would live with my son. I knew I didn't want him growing up in a metropolitan city like São Paulo.

I wasn't exactly surprised when a letter from Berry Smith Solicitors firm arrived for me in the post at my mother's house. The contents of this letter gave me great relief. Mark was not going to pursue custody of our child. His only request was to have a phone number and address so that he could speak to our boy on the phone and send him gifts in the post. The news gave me permission to seek a location to build a base for me and my son.

In January 2002, we visited friends in Cambuquira, a small town in Minas Gerais. And that's where I started a new phase in my life – a time for healing that started with forgiveness. It was also a time for expansion and growth, and as I metamorphosed into a new version of me, I needed a new chrysalis.

Rosa Ribeiro's House

We stayed with friends on their ranch on the outskirts of Cambuquira. Shortly after, I found work teaching English in the local primary school, so I rented a house in town. I also secured a contract with C. C. A. A. – a language school franchise where I'd trained to become an English teacher before I travelled to England with my university friend, Eliane Bandeira.

The property had an outbuilding where I would eventually start my school. Finally, my dreams were coming true, and I felt I was in charge of my life again. My landlady, Rosa, lived across the road and became one of my students and a friend I am still in touch with today. She has a beautiful heart and I can categorically say she has been one of the best landladies I have ever had. The other awesome one is Tracey Holloway, who gets a shout out later in this chapter.

Living in Cambuquira was so incredible I could write a whole book about it, but here are the highlights:

- Got a job teaching English at a local primary school;
- Moved into a lovely home with an outbuilding and a large back garden where we could pick our own mangos, persimmons, figs, grapes, oranges and jabuticabas (a fragrant and fragile small fruit that grows on the tree trunk);
- Started teaching English at a private language school in the town of Três Corações (Three Hearts), where Pelé was born - just to give you an interesting fact about it;
- Secured a one full day contract, teaching English using my method, at a Waldorf School (education approach founded by Rudolf Steiner), where my son joined as a student, and my very own assistant, since he was fluent in English;
- Had my 40th birthday surrounded by my family and friends (rather than feeling lonely, which was the case in Wales);

- Launched Baby Talks English School for Children & Young People (although I taught adults too) at the outbuilding in my back garden;

- Deepened my spiritual practice and met lots of interesting new people;

- Gave talks about personal development;

- Appeared in the local newspapers;

- Conceived the idea of writing A Book About Us: Celebrating Diversity, which would be published ten years later.

In Cambuquira, my son could enjoy the childhood taken away from him at the age of four, when he was forced to start formal 'schooling'. Thanks to the climate in Brazil, school buildings are used twice and thrice daily for different cohorts. My son went to school very early in the morning, came home at lunchtime and had the rest of the day to play and be a child. He would climb trees, swim in rivers and lakes, and go fishing with his friends. We enjoyed the Street Carnival, and watched the 2002 World Cup games on a big screen at the town's High Street, in the midst of all the shops and restaurants.

Cambuquira had frequent folklore parties, and my son made many friends, with whom he had tons of fun. Just after his 8th birthday, he asked if he could go to the nearby shops by himself. I remember watching him go off without me for the first time. His first taste of independence was a big step for both of us.

While deepening my spirituality, I did much forgiveness work. As part of my healing process, I worked on forgiving Mark and also forgiving myself. As a couple, we didn't communicate harmoniously, nor did we meet each other's needs. I can't know what was going on for Mark, but I knew I had to leave. I couldn't keep living in fear and unhappiness. Still, he was my son's father, and I couldn't ignore this fact. As the Christmas holidays approached, I had an idea to share with my son.

"Hey darling, come here for a minute. I got an idea I'd like to talk to you about."

"What is it, Mum?"

"How would you like Daddy to come over for Christmas?"

"Oh, yeah! Did he say he is coming?"

"No, I have yet to ask him. But we can call and invite him. Would you like to do that?"

"Yes, please! Can we call him now??"

We'd been in Brazil for over a year, and my life had swung a full 180 degrees into a meaningful, fulfilling, and enjoyable lifestyle. Inviting Mark to come and visit felt the right thing to do.

A week before Christmas 2002, we both made our way to Guarulhos International Airport. I could feel my son's excitement as we waited for his father to emerge from the Arrivals tunnel. My son's ear-to-ear grin matched Mark's as he walked toward our child. When he saw his son sneak through the barriers and start running toward him, Mark dropped all of his luggage and caught our boy in his arms. When it was my turn to hug him, I whispered "Thank you for coming" in his right ear.

When the time was right, I wanted Mark and I to have a heart-to-heart talk. In the meantime, many members of my family came over from the big city to spend Christmas with us in the countryside. We hired a lovely space with a swimming pool to accommodate everyone (it is summertime in Brazil in December) and we had one of the best Christmases ever!

The perfect moment arose for Mark and I to talk. We put all our differences aside and agreed to work from the premise of keeping our son's best interests, well-being, and happiness at heart. There was no question that my son was happy in Brazil and that what I was offering him had no resemblance to the lifestyle we had in Wales. Mark agreed for us to remain in Brazil and, fortunately, did not drag us into family courts. He suggested I take our son to England to visit him and spend the summer holidays together every year, so in June of the following year, I took my son to spend the holidays with his father. Little did I know that trip would change everything. Again…

In late July 2003, we flew to Wales, where I was visiting Arthur Benbow, the man who had become my father figure as well as a former landlord. He greeted us at Cardiff International Airport. Mark also wanted to spend time in Wales, where he'd grown up and where his mother still lived. The day after our arrival, I borrowed Arthur's car and took my son to meet his dad. They would be spending a whole month together, including his 9th birthday (the first one I would miss).

I parked the car at Bridgend Rail Station. The London train had already pulled in. My son opened the car door as soon as I had parked and stepped out, leaving the door wide open. When I saw my son running towards his father, I felt the joy of their embrace flood my heart. We did the handover quickly as I didn't want to open any conversation we couldn't complete. There was no animosity – only pure love and gratitude for each other and for our child. I kissed and hugged my son and said: "Have fun with Daddy, darling. Say hello to grandmother Iris for me."

I drove back to Arthur's cottage, where I had some time to reflect.

My soul had a message for me.

I couldn't quite grasp the implications of what I was being asked to do, but I remember thinking:

'Goodness, what am I doing? Mark and I conceived this child consciously. We both wanted to become parents. I have no right to bring my son up so far away from his dad.'

And just like that, I found myself at yet another significant crossroad.

My life was going so well in Brazil. What was I going to do? I surrendered to my soul, checked in with my heart and decided, there and then, that I should return to Wales so my son could maintain a close relationship with his father.

My mind was going: *'Wh@t???'*

And my heart said: *'Yep.'*

I left my son with his father, flew back to Brazil, and announced to my family I was leaving again. I sold most of what I had purchased to furnish an entire home, gave away what I couldn't sell, gave short notice to my landlady (who completely got where I was coming from) resigned from all my work engagements, packed, said goodbye to my family and friends for the second time, and returned to Wales.

My whole family thought I had lost the plot. However, I knew it was the right thing to do and that I had to do it. I have always trusted my inner guidance, even if it didn't always work the way I might have preferred. But I was well enough and no longer depressed, so I jumped right in. For two years, my son had a beautiful childhood where he could walk barefoot on sacred soil, climb trees, and fish in the local rivers. I was healed and felt strong again. One thought had crossed my reluctant mind as I was packing to leave my home country again:

'If I stay, when my son is old enough, he might resent me and leave me to live with his father. I can't bear the idea of my son losing faith and trust in me.'

And with that, at the Aeroporto Internacional de Guarulhos, I once more waved goodbye to everything familiar and close to me.

Back in Wales!

September 2003

A helping hand at Granary Cottage

I had no home, job and hardly any money left with all the flights back and forth. Arthur, my "adopted British dad", had paid us a visit in Brazil in January 2003 and stayed with us in Cambuquira. When we arrived in Wales, he was kind enough to give hospitality to my son and me at the lovely Ty Isha Farm cottage he had rented after his travels. We stayed there for a couple of months. It was a serene and peaceful spot with beautiful walking paths and a lake nearby decorated with water lilies.

April Cottage, another stepping stone

Arthur's cottage was let out as he had been cycling abroad again. However, his tenants were leaving in November, so the three of us moved back to April Cottage. *'At least some familiarity,'* I thought, as I enjoyed that cottage's safe and cosy feel in a village near Cowbridge, the main local town in the Vale of Glamorgan. Only this time, the furniture was no longer mine, and my cat Max stayed in Brazil, where our neighbours in Cambuquira happily adopted him.

Arthur was off to India and Nepal on a bike tour for Christmas and the New Year, so my son and I had the place to ourselves until I sought out work and found a place for us to live. I had noticed the smallest cottage on the grounds of Ty Isha Farm the time we had taken temporary shelter at the Granary Cottage, so when Arthur returned from his trip, my son and I moved into the one-bedroom studio unit. It was all I could afford.

The Stables, Ty Isha Farm, Bonvilston

In February 2004, I rented the Stables so my son and I could have privacy. There were no cooking facilities - only a small area to make tea, coffee, and snacks (no oven), so I used to travel to April Cottage to cook our meals. Arthur loved my cooking, so it worked well for him too. My son was attending school by then, and I decided to return to college.

My language business had obviously folded and even though I could revive it, I felt ready for a new career. I needed to reinvent myself, and do something more meaningful. After getting career guidance at the local job centre, I took their advice and enrolled at Bridgend College to take an access course as a pathway for a university degree in counselling.

Living at the Stables was no longer practical since I didn't have a car, so I rented a house in Cowbridge, near my son's school and where I could have access to public transport to commute to college.

Settling down at Aubrey Terrace

After hopping from place to place, it was time to settle and put some roots down. Both my son and I needed stability. I got a grant to study, which allowed me to remain a full-time mum as my education timetable worked in tandem with my son's.

Initially, we moved to number three of a row of seven houses called Aubrey Terrace. Then after about a year, number four next door became available. It was a more spacious two-bedroom house and had a bigger kitchen, a gorgeous big bathroom, another bathroom downstairs with a pantry cupboard and a cat flap! Sheena, the five-year-old cat we adopted from a shelter, moved in before we did! So, it was a no brainer and the move was the easiest I have ever tackled.

At college, I put my name forward to have personal counselling again, and fully committed to the inner work. Whilst in Brazil, I had emotional support from family and friends, but I needed to talk with a professional about specific trauma-related matters.

Three grounded and focused years later, in September 2007, I was offered a place at the University of Glamorgan to undergo a counselling degree. Uncannily, this had formerly been the Polytechnic of Wales, where I taught the Portuguese language intensive to law undergraduates seventeen years ago. (The University of Glamorgan has since had a merger with Newport University. It is now the University of South Wales.)

I had aimed to become a school-based counsellor, knowing I wanted to empower children and young people, especially after the suicide incidents involving 26 young people in the Bridgend Borough between 2007 and 2008.

After graduating in 2010, I secured a post with Barnardo's, one of the counselling service providers, and I worked as a face-to-face counsellor at a couple of schools in my area. I practised for three years until I burned out, primarily due to a misalignment between my efforts to offer alternatives to complement my practice and the school's rigid environment.

Most of my clients were experiencing self-harming behaviours and suicidal ideation. They all lacked emotional resilience, as the education system neglects this critical aspect of human development.

Please know that I am not here to point fingers and criticise, but the misalignment had in part to do with the fact that students were referred to the counselling room as if it was a punishment. Most students that came to my room were 'sent' there rather than given an informed choice. This meant they were initially reluctant to come, and it was up to me to educate them on how to make the most of the service. I am proud of my results, though. My burnout was more connected with how the service operated rather than the caseload. My personal experiences surrounding suicide made me even more determined to solve this agonising problem we face in our human journey.

So, I created a solution using a four-petaled flower.

Original drawing of the Living Flower

In chapter four, you will meet Jaz, a sixteen-year-old determined to end her life. I will share the Living Flower metaphor and technique I created to work with suicidal clients.

Meanwhile, let me continue my journey as a context for writing this book.

From Breakthrough to Sovereignty

2012-2023

After living at Aubrey Terrace in Cowbridge for eight years, in January 2012 we moved to Geraint's Way, a bigger house in the outskirts of the small market town. I had started a private practice working with adult clients on top of my school-based counselling contract, and had started creating my own holistic approach to emotional wellness. During my degree, I felt inspired to create content and decided to refrain from reading other professional and academic books in my field. In May 2012 I published *A Book About Us – Celebrating Diversity*, to be used in schools to raise self-awareness and promote emotional literacy. This is the book idea originally conceived at the time I lived in Cambuquira. Unfortunately, my work was rejected by senior management of the schools where I practised as a face-to-face counsellor, and by most schools I approached. I started feeling despondent and unfulfilled.

When my son had turned nineteen, he became independent and got himself a job and a place to live. One day, he sat me down to talk about his plans to pursue new work.

"Hey Mum, I just wanted to take this moment to thank you for all you have done for me. In particular, I would like to thank you for your sacrifices. I have the most amazing memories of our time in Brazil, but I am genuinely grateful that you brought me back to Wales so I could have a close relationship with Dad. I can only imagine how hard it must have been for you to leave your family and friends for the second time. The lifestyle you created for us in Cambuquira was incredible, and I had lots of fun. It must have been tough for you to walk away from it and say goodbye to Brazil again. I am so proud of you. I love you so much, and I needed you to know how much I appreciate you."

"Wow, darling. Thank you so much for recognising that. I didn't do any of it expecting anything from you. I did it because it was the right thing to do by you and your father, but to hear you say that and know that I was right in listening to my heart's whisper makes it all worthwhile. You are an incredible young man, and I am so proud of you. Well done for getting this work opportunity. I am sure you will do extremely well. I am not ready to see you leave me yet, but I have raised you to be independent and find your pearl in life. I love you so much. You can count on me for anything. I will always be here for you, and I look forward to seeing you fulfill your potential and find happiness in life."

As I watched my boy pack his belongings and embark on his independent life journey, I felt the need to flap my wings and take off, too. I decided to resign from my post as a school-based counsellor and move up north, where my friend and adopted dad had moved. Once again, I sold my furniture, gave everything else away to charity, packed my bags and left Wales for an adventure in England.

Settling in Settle

Arthur had sold April Cottage to continue his cycling

adventures and moved to Settle, a breathtaking piece of land in North Yorkshire, in the north of England. He had met a 'lady friend.' He had also set up a charity to support education in Nepal, a country he visited often, and I had also become involved in the project.

So, before I left Wales, I did a sky jump, raising about £1000 for Kids at School in Nepal (http://kasin.org.uk), and then made my way north. I spent a few months with Arthur at his fabulous apartment, then rented a little cottage nearby.

Starting all over again at Caxton Cottage, Settle

In addition to finding myself nestled in the stunning beauty of what is known as God's own country, with the three peaks in Yorkshire Dales, Settle offered me an opportunity to have what felt like a family life, with Arthur as my father figure. I felt grounded and motivated to start a new counselling practice, and to approach the local schools to deliver the self-awareness and emotional literacy workshops I had created.

I did a book launch, gave a talk at Settle Victoria Hall, and delivered two of my workshops, *The Living Flower* and *The Life Box*, at a local primary school.

I walked the three peaks: Pen-y-ghent, Ingleborough, and Whernside, and raised more money for KASIN. All was going well until my son told me he wasn't happy.

It was 2015, and he had been working very, very hard. I am thrilled he was self-aware enough to realise something was wrong and that he was becoming depressed. He worked as a

Junior Sous Chef at a Michelin Star Restaurant in South Wales – a busy and prestigious kitchen. On his feet for hours every day, and with no time for social life, he realised he needed a break. We had a long discussion, and together, we decided to create an opportunity for him to go to Brazil to live and work. This would also give me the opportunity to finally return to my birth land, too.

'Woohoo!' I thought to myself. *I'm finally going home!*

Then Arthur made an announcement.

"I'm off to New Zealand for six months on a home exchange. Would you like to come?"

The funny thing is, New Zealand had been coming to my radar on and off since I started working as a counsellor. It kept popping up, in conversation, adverts, and other bizarre ways.

'Is this another sign the Universe is giving me? What is it about New Zealand that is calling my soul? I need to go and investigate. I'll go to New Zealand, then to Brazil and join my son and my family. For good this time!'

A friend asked me if I could mind her home and Toulouse, the cat she kindly adopted when I left Wales, as she would be spending three months in Spain. I packed my bags and left Settle to take residence in Cardiff, where I had no rent to pay and could be near my son before he left. Plus, all the money I made I could save for my trip to New Zealand and Brazil.

My cousin Luciano offered my son a job and a place to live, and off he went.

I planned my trip to New Zealand via Turkey to visit a friend, then Nepal, where I would spend a month volunteering (2015 was the year a massive earthquake devastated the country). From there I would go to Malaysia for a short break enroute to Wellington, where I would join Arthur and welcome 2016 in Paraparaumu, Kapiti, New Zealand.

The three months in New Zealand could only be described as 'paradise on Earth.' The exceptional beauty of the land blew me away. Arthur and I stayed at Kapiti, in the North Island about an hour's drive or train journey to Wellington. We stayed in a house that belonged to a man named Bryan, who would eventually become a good friend.

I intended to contact the local schools and do a book signing event, but it was their summer holidays, so instead, I went into holiday mode, too. Considering everything I had gone through over the past 27 years, I deserved an extended break, with no rent or bills to pay. I had a couple of counselling clients working online, which covered my personal expenses.

I found Zumba classes to attend, where I met Kat, the Zumba instructor. She encouraged me to take the training to become an instructor, but I thought nothing of it at the time.

March 2016 came around very quickly (time does go fast when you are having fun) and it was time for me to make my way back to Brazil, join my son, and start my life all over again.

When I arrived in São Paulo, my son told me that he was planning to return to Wales after all. Although he was doing well and was enjoying his work and all that Brazil had to offer, he was missing Wales. A month later, my family and I are waving goodbye to him at Guarulhos International Airport.

One day, out of the blue, I saw an advert on Facebook to do the Zumba training. I signed up, just for fun. After three months of quality time with my family, and helping to look after my elderly parents, I too decided to return to Wales. I couldn't contemplate living so far away from my only child. I love my family dearly, but similar to taking my son back to the U.K. to be near his father all those years ago, I also needed to be near him.

So, in June 2016, with no home or job, I returned to Wales once again.

In July, after spending a few weeks with a friend, I moved in with an elderly lady who lived in Droitwich in the Midlands, England and became her care provider. I was no longer a member of BACP (British Association of Counselling and Psychotherapy), so I could no longer practise counselling. I planned to pursue my writing career whilst caring for Helen, whose mental capacity and physical mobility were quickly deteriorating. Her three daughters would take turns covering so I could have a break, but it became a struggle for me to cope, as she didn't want another care provider involved.

Then an opportunity arose for me to teach Zumba at the local Leisure Centre where I had been going as a participant. I took it, as Zumba had become integral to my well-being. To earn a living from it was very appealing, so after six months of caring for Helen, although very heartwarming, I realized it wasn't sustainable. I gave my notice, found a room in a shared house, focused on teaching Zumba and never looked back. Today,

Zumba is part of my holistic approach to wellness.

This is when my nomadic life as a spiritual butterfly really took off. Quite unintentionally, all the living possibilities I created didn't work out. I had all sorts of peculiar experiences, including waking up one morning to find my landlord stark naked, vacuuming the lounge!

All in all, I went from one place to another – five to be exact, in less than a year – unable to settle. I have a set of standards I am not prepared to compromise, so although at first the properties and private spaces I looked at appeared adequate, issues related to poor management and low standards always emerged. The majority of homeowners seemed happy enough to take my money, but weren't exactly committed to my well being as far as hygiene and disruptive behaviour was concerned. As a result, I lived like a gypsy for a year, going from one spot to the next, not finding joy anywhere.

At the time, my son was living in Cardiff with his then-girlfriend, a New Zealander who had immigrated to Wales when she was young. I felt pushed aside, unable to see my son much as his girlfriend always found an excuse for me not to visit. Things weren't working well, and I started to feel depressed again. I was tired of moving around, and winter was around the corner. In December 2017, I went to Brazil to spend Christmas with my family and stayed there for four months, re-evaluating my life and considering a plan to move forward.

In May 2018, Arthur had a proposition for me. He had plans to go to America and Canada on various home exchanges. He asked if I would manage the Airbnb at his apartment in Settle for a couple of months, which meant no rent to pay, and the possibility of joining him afterwards since the apartment would have to be accessible for home exchange visitors during July and August. So mid May, I returned to Settle.

After two months of managing his Airbnb guests, I met Arthur in Los Angeles. From California, we travelled to Ashland and Portland, Oregon. Then we flew to Canada and spent some time in Nanaimo, Vancouver Island. We visited our mutual friend Christine Tingle on the sunshine coast of British Columbia, then made our way to Montreal before returning to England in early September.

Back in God's own country, I started working as a care provider until I found my feet again. Before long, I had five sources of income, including working as a Specialist Educator working with a young person who had been excluded from mainstream school. I loved it. I was able to create my own curriculum and in collaboration with the young person, we designed and implemented some cool educational projects. We all learn so much more effectively when we feel inspired by the things we love doing and are met with enthusiasm and support from our educators. I love teaching provided the content I am teaching is what I am passionate about: Self-awareness and Emotional Literacy.

Things were going well financially, although I was out working most days for long hours at a time. I rented a cottage in Giggleswick (yes, that is the village's name) just outside Settle. However, some underlying unresolved issues still existed. The loneliness grabbed me again, and the alcohol misuse reared its ugly head. I also began using work as a coping mechanism again. My life was not working. I needed to do some soul-searching.

New Zealand was still on my radar. I contacted my friend Bryan and asked if I could go and visit, as I was compelled to do some research to carry on with my book series *A Book About Us: Celebrating Diversity*. I was also writing an online course. To my delight, he said I would be very welcome.

In December 2019, I arrived in Paraparaumu for the second time. I didn't know what to expect or why New Zealand was calling me, but I decided to listen to my heart and fulfill its call.

During my time there, I learned that New Zealand has one of the highest suicide rates. In fact, according to a report by Unicef, New Zealand has the highest youth suicide rate by far in the developed world. It was such a bewildering shock to learn that a place of such astounding beauty could have a suicide rate twice as high as the U.S. rate and almost five times that of Britain.

As I read those statistics, my heart sank, and I felt the urgency of my soul's calling. My work visa and money were running out, so in March 2020, I flew back to the U.K. A few days after I arrived, the whole world went into Covid lockdown.

Everything had come to a halt, and the fear amongst people was palpable. We had to stay home, wear masks, disinfect our shopping, keep a distance from people, and only go out for the essentials.

I got into lockdown with some friends in Brighton, on the south coast of England, but I couldn't go anywhere. No one could. Everyone seemed terrified of getting contaminated with the so-called virus. It was all very bizarre.

When the first lockdown ended in May 2020, I travelled to Manchester and stayed at my friend's flat until I found a more permanent place in Wales to stay near my son.

Lying Low at Lodge Cottage

I moved to the cosiest, friendliest and most functional place I have ever rented in a small village at the Vale of Glamorgan in South Wales. It wasn't far from Cowbridge, where I had lived before with my son. My landlady, Tracey Holloway, was a kind, generous, approachable person with a big heart. I want to give her a special 'shout out' for trusting me enough to lend me some money to buy a new laptop. Thanks to Tracey, I am writing this book.

Due to the health crisis, I could not resume working in the community or with young people, along with thousands, if not millions, of people who lost their jobs or were forced to stay at home. The government encouraged us to sign up to get Universal Credit, for which I was grateful. It meant I could focus on my writing and my spiritual development. I started to research many aspects of life that didn't make sense to me.

Tracey's cottage was serene, peaceful and safe. Perfect for writing.

Collaborating with other professionals, I contributed to two books: *The Everyday Girl's Guide to Living in Truth, Self-love & Acceptance,* and the best-selling *She Speaks Her Truth: Women's Words Changing the World.*

Unfortunately, Tracey needed the cottage back after she put her bungalow on the market, and gave me notice to move out. So, sad to be leaving, I accepted the change with serenity, trusting that the Universe would find me yet another chrysalis for my next phase of transformation. I posted on the village's Facebook group and surrendered to the outcome. Within a day or so, I got a direct message from a property owner with a furnished empty house needing a tenant to make it their home. In March 2021, I was in my new space, with lovely front and back gardens, and sunrise and sunset views.

Writing My Manuscript at Monk's Court Cottage

The idyllic cottage stood just outside the village, and there I learned to grow some vegetables, sowed 33 sunflower seeds, and celebrated my 60th birthday amongst friends that have become my adopted British family.

Most importantly, however, it's where I wrote this manuscript.

I have realised that I came to this planet to write, and I believe my life's purpose is to write and publish the messages in this book. It has taken me two different careers to get here, but here I am, fulfilling my soul's mission.

I have fallen in love with the whole process: from working through the resistance of writing this content to the tangible possibility of seeing my creation doing its own work in the lives of those it will touch.

My message may be triggering for a lot of people. But as I said before, this is my truth. I am compelled to share with those who are ready to receive it. And as I tackle the process of reliving my most painful memories, I trust it will serve as the context required for you, my reader, to embrace its message.

And as I draw this chapter to a close, I invite you to stay open. This is my story – my version of the truth about the sacredness of human life.

We are all unique individuals with our own unique stories to tell. What connects us to each other is the power of the emotions that touch our hearts so that we can feel each other's pain as well as joy. Our ability to empathise is what makes us truly human. All my travels to distinctly diverse countries, landscapes and cultures allowed me to recognise that the emotional threads connecting our human hearts to each other have no boundaries. Love and compassion see no skin colour or personal beliefs. It is available to all, regardless of age or sexual orientation. That's how we are able to practice empathy. The lack of empathy is what leads us away from our own souls, away from our hearts, and away from each other. This lack makes us capable of going against the Natural Law that governs us, to harm and destroy instead of love and enhance.

In Chapter 3, I invite you to embark on the personal development aspect of this book and allow your soul to explore new ways of being, thinking, doing, and experiencing life. I will close this narrative with three letters:

Letter to Mark

Dear Mark (not his real name),

It has been 25 years since we went our separate ways.

You are a married man now and even inherited grandchildren. I am very happy for you.

Our son is 29, but we are not growing old together as you promised. It's okay, though. We both learned a lot since then, plus everything happens for a reason and being single all these years was necessary for me to become the person I am today.

I wish I could have written a letter to you all those years ago explaining why I felt the need to leave the way I did. I am genuinely sorry for the heartache that it caused you. I could not see any other way to deal with what I was going through then, and I doubt if I would still be here if I hadn't.

However, in the depth of my being, my actions had our son's best interest at heart as I was too vulnerable and didn't want to do anything I couldn't undo and potentially scar our child for the rest of his life. I am proud that I found the strength to take the necessary actions before it was too late.

As for our separation, I am sorry it ended the way it did. I needed to defend myself as deep down, I was scared shitless. The truth is, I was afraid of you, and I couldn't take the abuse any longer. I had to defend myself and bring our son up in a harmonious environment. I am sorry we didn't manage to find a happy medium to resolve our issues.

I read relationship books, went back to college, and had therapy to understand you, but you wouldn't listen. The more I stood up to defend and speak my truth, the angrier and more intimidating you got. Your verbal abuse was like emotional torture and so hurtful. All I wanted was for us to learn how to love each other unconditionally by accepting each other's points of view. I do not subscribe to violence of any kind. Words can hurt deeper than physical abuse. That was not love on your part, and I wasn't willing to compromise my sovereignty.

I resented you for throwing mine and Roger's letters away when I was in Brazil with our son. How dare you violate such a personal treasure? You had no right!

I believe and live by Natural Law which says, 'Do No Harm'. Plain and simple. Harm comes under many guises; the verbal one is sneaky and detrimental. Touching my personal belongings without my permission was dishonest of you, and I lost trust.

You're a decent man. You have a good heart. I know you do, and I love you for that. You're a loving father, and our son loves you very much. But the way you treated me back then wasn't loving. Becoming a lone parent was the last thing I wanted for myself. I wouldn't have agreed to conceive a child with you if I had any idea our relationship would end this way.

I am sorry I couldn't be the submissive woman you perhaps needed me to be. I am a free-spirited, independent human being. My mother was my greatest role model; she taught me to stand on my own two feet and be true to myself. I will never compromise my soul.

I cannot control what happens in life from an external point of view. I had no control over your actions, but I am responsible for responding to situations that affect me. I didn't want our child to grow up in our relationship's tense environment. Even years after the separation, you still undermined me and played mind games. I don't subscribe to that either. I had to do something. It took a drastic move on my part, and I am sorry you stood at Bridgend train station waiting for our son the day we left. I couldn't take chances of you finding out what I was going to do. I had to coordinate everything and think of every detail.

On the other hand, thank you for giving me the best gift life could ever give me. I remember when you turned to me at a Sport's Day once and said you could not have chosen a better woman to be the mother of your child. I appreciate you saying that. And I also appreciate you for being my son's father.

We had a great time together when we first met. I'm very fond of the memories we created before our son came along. So I'm sorry. I'm sorry I wasn't the woman you wanted me to be. I have a duty to be who and what I truly am and never compromise or sell my soul for anything or anybody.

I am glad that you found happiness. It means different things to different people. My happiness leans more on satisfying my soul's purpose. But who knows, one day, I too can find the love and companionship of a man who can honour and accept me for who I am.

Thank you, Mark!

Be well,

Stay well,

Stay happy,

Eliana

Letter to My Son

My darling son,

I am so proud of the human being you are stepping into.

I love watching your continued growth and being the best version of yourself that you choose to experience. We are on a never-ending life journey, and I am thrilled that our paths are intertwined.

I am profoundly proud of the man that you are. You are far more than I could have wished for as a son. You will always be the beautiful, funny, articulate, curious and self-assured boy I remember you being.

All the travels, the moves, and the uncertainties that delineated our paths as I navigated motherhood as a lone parent never phased you. By the time you were nineteen, we had moved houses twelve times and lived in seven different locations and in two very different Countries!

You were always ready for an adventure. We had so much fun together, and I am so thankful you could embark on the lifeship I was steering with as much ease and grace I could muster.

You are ethical. You are honest. You are a hard-working individual and an asset to any society.

You started working when you were twelve years old. I couldn't afford to give you pocket money, so you got a Saturday job plucking weeds out of my friend's garden. You earned £5.00, and you were so proud of yourself for having your own money, so you could go and spend on sweets and save for other things you wanted.

You got so excited when you managed to save £20 to buy the Simpson

Chessboard you had seen at The Rainbow Plaza in Llantwit Major, where we used to go most Fridays after school, regardless the weather. A seaside town in the Vale Of Glamorgan near Cowbridge where we lived for a few grounding and building years. It was our special Friday treat, and we looked forward to it. We would get chips and eat at the beach, even in winter. You loved looking for crabs in the rock pools.

So many sweet moments we shared while you were growing up.

This year you turn twenty-nine, and it's incredible to see you being the independent, well-functioning human being that you are. You have your work; you have your commitments. You keep your word, and you have no idea what it means for a mother to see her child out there in the world, navigating this challenging game we call life with a good degree of success. You are my best friend, and I love you so, so much.

I just needed to acknowledge you and speak from my soul in relation to the message of this book and to say how grateful I am for you holding space for me, even before I knew what holding space for someone meant. As I became a deliberate and conscious space holder for clients, I realize that you held space for me subliminally and so very tangibly.

You stepped in at the precise moment I was contemplating ending my life, like a Divine Intervention. You were five years old at the time, and I believe your soul guided you to look for me just then. It scares me to think of the consequences to your life had I gone ahead with the painkiller overdose. It horrifies me to imagine you going through the aftermath of my naive and uninformed decision to extinguish my light by ending my physical life.

It grieves me to know that millions or even billions of humans are unaware that their suffering is clouding their inner vision of who

86

and what they truly are. Hence this book. My experiences brought me here to tell my story and share my medicine.

You have a huge part to play in this, as I would not be here today if it weren't for you.

I believe I did my very best to be a good mother to you. My mother inspired me. She set the standards high, and I am so blessed I had her as my role model. My mother is an incredible woman, and in her almost 92 trips around the sun, she is still the beautiful and strong-hearted woman she carries in her soul.

There is something important I need to speak about. And that is alcohol.

I am so grateful, thankful and relieved that you did not fall into the same trap I fell into and that you are breaking the chain. I watched my dad go to the local bar where I grew up in the suburbs of São Paulo almost every day. I used to hate him for it, and meanwhile, I watched my mother work herself to the bone. I never thought his behaviour was a good example, but I have come to innerstand and forgive him as he navigated his life with the tool kit he was handed down.

I am not proud of having fallen into the same trap. I am not a pub goer, but I did misuse alcohol. I learned to do that from our culture as society sets its tone with well thought narratives and structures our lives.

I did it discreetly.

I did it alone.

You never really knew much about it as a child because you'd be in bed.

I did it in my own time, by myself, which is sad. It's very, very sad, and I am so relieved you didn't allow alcohol to trick you. It didn't entrap you in the ways that it does for so many of us. So many people around the globe have their lives touched by alcohol in a detrimental way.

I must speak to this in this space because the misuse of anything harms us. I like the teachings of the Buddha about finding the middle ground. Everything is okay in moderation. Everything you choose to do with your body and your life is okay within the boundaries of respecting and honouring yourself and those around you that are inevitably impacted by your actions.

We are here to experience life. We are Divine Souls having a human experience using this sacred body. You can choose to live your life whichever way you want. Provided that your actions do not detrimentally impact somebody else's life. That's all we have to be mindful of. Not simple, nor easy either, but it's a good guideline.

My mother taught me that my independence ends where somebody else's begins. The sermon she gave my eldest sister when I was twelve made much sense to me, and I did my best to live by its teachings.

My freedom of expression has the right to be expressed. I am only responsible for how I express myself. I cannot be responsible for how it is received. If people disagree with us, that's absolutely fine, but by the same token, no one can take our right away from expressing our truth. We all have the right – and responsibility – to speak our truth. Tactfully, compassionately, and from the heart, since 'truth' can be a bitter pill to swallow.

Truth brought me here to share this message with the world, so thank you for coming to my rescue when I most needed it.

When you were thirteen years old, you gave me a Mother's Day gift you bought with your own money that says: "If I could choose again, I'd still choose you!"

I feel so honoured, privileged and blessed that you did. I loved you even before I carried you in my womb. When I first held you in my arms and looked into your eyes, I was overcome with an indescribable feeling. I would like to think that, like my mother, I have set good examples for you, and I cannot wait to see you stepping into the role of the brilliant dad you have the potential to be.

You are the best of the best!

I love you,

Mum xxx

Letter from My Divine Soul:

Dear Eliana Regina,

I will keep this brief as there is so much you wish to share with your readers. However, I couldn't let you go any further before pausing to acknowledge you.

It may appear more attractive for the human mind to choose the quickest road and be tempted by shortcuts.

I am touched by your courage and commitment. Despite all the crossroads and complex decisions, you never wavered from following your heart. Your heart is your soul's voice. Your true voice. You got back on track whenever you swayed and got lost in the dramas of external circumstances.

Well done for your perseverance and for finding out who and what you truly are.

Thank you for listening and for integrating me as the essential aspect of your S.E.L.F. as a human.

I am so glad you noticed the rapeseed fields all around you, including your garden, as you finished this sacred piece of work.

It will be innerstood and embraced by those ready to receive it.

There is so much more we are going to co-create together.

Let's get to work!

With Unconditional Love,

Your Divine Soul

Like a Butterfly

Like a butterfly, I come and I go.
Like the waves of the cosmic sea,
I breathe in, and I breathe out.

Like a butterfly, I land and take flight.
Like the mountains and rivers in their glory,
I reside in infinite sight.

Like a butterfly, I flutter, and I settle.
Like the Divine Soul that birthed my body,
In the magic of its petals.

Like a chrysalis that creates her own wings,
An inner quest moves me
Ever close to what I came to find.

In search of my true essence,
To which I am aligned.
Letting go of false whispers that poison our minds!

BeTalks Books © 2023 ER

CHAPTER THREE

Our Divine Soul
Who We Are

Divine Soul, Sacred Body

In My Dreams

Flickering, flicker of *LIGHT*
Hovers over me throughout the night.

Waking my Spirit

Showing the Way...

> Free from all burdens,
> that chain my body and mind each day

In my dreams,
> *I awake*

In my dreams,
> *I can fly*

In my dreams,
> *I unlock*

What is Sacred,
> to release

> *The Divine*

Eliana Regina, April Cottage 2001

Divine Soul, Sacred Body

Chapter 3

We are divine, eternal, and infinite sparks of a Creator Source, having a tangible and heartfelt experience in a sacred human body on a physical planet we call Earth.

In this chapter, I will focus on that spark as I take you on a journey to discover Who We Are, according to my experiences, observations, and conclusions about Who I Am.

My quest to make sense of who I am and what I am doing here on this challenging planet propelled me to embark on the path to quench my thirst to know myself.

I commune and work with this incredible, alive, magical energy force as I play with creating a more deliberate and conscious reality.

The above poem came to me after a series of recurring dreams in which I felt my soul hovering above my body while I was asleep. It was scary initially because I felt like I was going up on a high-speed lift (elevator). The sensation woke me up, but the same thing happened the following night and the night after that.

In the dream, if I can call it a dream, I merged with what I can only describe as an infinite field. I couldn't see it, but I felt it. I felt my soul poised over my physical body, asleep in bed, but at the same time, I was in a whole different dimension. My soul was flickering about like a candle flame. By the second night, I was no longer frightened. A wave of peace washed over my being, and I felt whole.

I remember waking up the following morning feeling as if the Holy Spirit had touched me.

When I went to bed the third night, I wished for that encounter with my soul again. When I felt the high-speed sensation, it became even more potent. I could linger in that blissful state and was reassured that our Spiritual Nature is benevolent, loving, compassionate, eternal, infinite, and incredibly delightful. It is divine.

When I woke up from the third encounter with my soul, my mind compelled me to write down a stream of words that became the poem above.

I realised that human beings are a spark of the Divine and that spark, flicker, or fractal is our individual soul. Therefore, I concluded our soul is Divine. And if the flicker is made of Light, based on the streams of words downloaded onto my consciousness, then it is fair to assume that the creative source, whence we originate from, is light in its purest form.

As I started meditating on my experience and conclusions,

I joined some dots and came up with answers to my burning questions about who and what I am.

Contrary to being told by my family's religion that I was born a sinner and, as such, dirty and of dark tendencies, I thought of a definition for our soul which resonated with the very core of my being as truth:

Source

Of

Unique

Light

Light! I am made of light!

The soul is for the individual self, whilst Spirit is its creative source of origin.

What remained for me to explore, to integrate that inner knowing entirely, was the concept of **light.**

I remembered the Bible's suggestion:

"In the beginning was the word..." (or you can think of the Big Bang if you are more scientifically minded)

Eureka!

It is all about **sound!**

Sounds create vibrations.

Vibrations have specific frequencies that go on to emit **light.**

Light splits into colours, and colours form geometrical shapes, like beautiful mandalas.

Aha! Our soul is made of light and came from the Universal Force that desired to experience Itself through infinite possibilities, in different forms, represented by all earthly kingdoms.

Light is the sweet spot of creation, and one of these conceived forms is the human body. The miraculous miracle of all miracles! The human body is the gift of creation to carry our souls so Spirit can be made flesh as you and I. It's genius. Absolute genius!

Light is awareness in the flesh. And awareness is the presence of consciousness.

Fascinating! Truly fascinating. This means we can touch 'light' with our awareness; in doing so, we are technically connecting with our Maker to the degree to which we raise our self-awareness. This is a beautiful thing.

But wait a minute, why does humanity seem to be experiencing the opposite of that?

The concept of light for me makes me think of radiance, glow, joy, delight, luminescence, brightness, brilliance, beauty, and many more uplifting ways of being.

Unless you live on a different planet than me, everything looks dark, dense, heavy, hostile, confused, broken and distorted.

Why is that?

Well, reality arises in language, and what is language, if not streams of sounds?

Words create worlds. So we must pay attention to the 'sounds' we consume, be it words, music, thoughts, or ideas.

Please note the statement above, which will become very relevant in the next chapter.

For now, let's refocus our attention on our soul. I know intuitively and experientially, during my dream state, that my soul is a spark of the Divine. Call it Source, Universal Force, Creator, Architect, Mother Father God, or whatever you resonate with the most.

I like the word Divine as it has some different connotations running through its meaning. As a Portuguese speaker, the Latin 'divinare' (foresee) makes the word even more attractive, as it gives me a sense of accomplishment for having intuitively discovered who I am.

I knew I didn't need a middleman to access this God Source. I was right in questioning the teachings of organised religions and carving my own spiritual path.

So how can the soul assist us in living as human beings navigating life in order to evolve and thrive?

Existentially speaking, humans operate on four levels of experience. I will demonstrate this by inviting you to interact with this content.

The four existential worlds we construct our realities and experience life with are:

1. The Physical (using our bodies and experiencing our environment)
2. The Personal (employing our mental abilities to create and navigate life)
3. The Social (engaging with people in our lives and society in general)
4. The Spiritual (connecting with our true essence and bathing in its sovereignty)

The above is based on the contributions of German philosophers Martin Heidegger and Swiss psychiatrist Ludwig Binswanger in the late 19th and early 20th centuries, coined initially as:

1. Umwelt - the natural world around us
2. Eigenwelt - our own subjective world (our thoughts and feelings)
3. Mitwelt - refers to being in the world with other people
4. Uberwelt - the spiritual or metaphysical dimension.

On the following page, you will see a four-petalled flower.

This flower is the original metaphor I created at the beginning of my career as a counsellor. We will use this as a template for you, the reader, to engage with the text.

At the centre of the flower, please write the word: **Soul.**

Then choose one petal and write the word: **Inspiration.**

When exploring the word inspiration, we find it means 'the drawing in of the breath; inhalation but also divine influence, a sudden brilliant or timely idea and the quality of being inspired.' I think of inspiration as 'filled or informed with Spirit.'

Now choose another petal and write the word: **Purpose.**

I was very young when I heard myself asking: *'What is the purpose of my being here on this planet? What am I doing here?'*

These are essential existential questions that persisted throughout my life. They gave me a sense of direction. I didn't know what my purpose was for a long time, but I knew I was following the breadcrumbs that would lead me to the answer. One often makes a connection to a career path that is, ideally, aligned with what you are passionate about. I was passionate about foreign languages, hence my first career focused on that.

I have finally come to attune with my true purpose. I am grateful that my two previous careers have served as playgrounds for exercising my mental and emotional muscles to be fit for this one – writing and sharing this message.

What are YOU passionate about?

What gives you a sense of direction?

Where is your soul leading you?

How is your idea of purpose showing up in your life?

Each of us has an individual purpose in whatever capacity, but ultimately, as a collective, we are all here to serve each other by sharing our gifts and talents with one another so that together, we can thrive.

On a third petal, please write: **Virtues.**

Virtues form the essence of someone's character. They are behaviours that show high moral standards. Simply put, they are your qualities.

Some virtues I praise myself for are creativity, commitment, enthusiasm, courage, honesty, integrity, and my passion for personal growth.

What virtues are you most aligned with?

What shines through as your character's endowments?

What virtues would you like to invest time and effort in?

On the remaining petal, please write **Self-expression.**

Soul Flower

We are all here to express ourselves as we experience life. We are free and sovereign beings, and we don't need anyone's permission to speak our truths and step into our power.

We don't need a queen or a king to rule over us, and we certainly don't need a government to tell us what to do or what and how to think. Conscientious human beings can choose what is best for themselves and their children.

We do, however, need the appropriate guidance. My guidance came mostly from my soul, and I trust her unconditionally. It has taken me years of inner work and self-development to come up with some answers, and I am here to share them with you.

The kind of information I found in my search along the way has helped me make sense of the truth hidden under societal conditioning and assisted me in advancing and expanding my innerstanding of who and what I am.

I trust the which follows will help you, too, especially if you have never come across this knowledge.

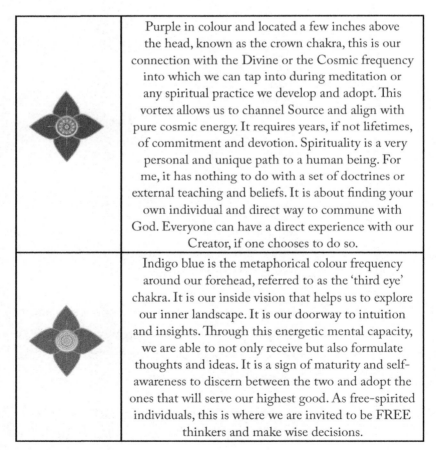

	Purple in colour and located a few inches above the head, known as the crown chakra, this is our connection with the Divine or the Cosmic frequency into which we can tap into during meditation or any spiritual practice we develop and adopt. This vortex allows us to channel Source and align with pure cosmic energy. It requires years, if not lifetimes, of commitment and devotion. Spirituality is a very personal and unique path to a human being. For me, it has nothing to do with a set of doctrines or external teaching and beliefs. It is about finding your own individual and direct way to commune with God. Everyone can have a direct experience with our Creator, if one chooses to do so.
	Indigo blue is the metaphorical colour frequency around our forehead, referred to as the 'third eye' chakra. It is our inside vision that helps us to explore our inner landscape. It is our doorway to intuition and insights. Through this energetic mental capacity, we are able to not only receive but also formulate thoughts and ideas. It is a sign of maturity and self-awareness to discern between the two and adopt the ones that will serve our highest good. As free-spirited individuals, this is where we are invited to be FREE thinkers and make wise decisions.

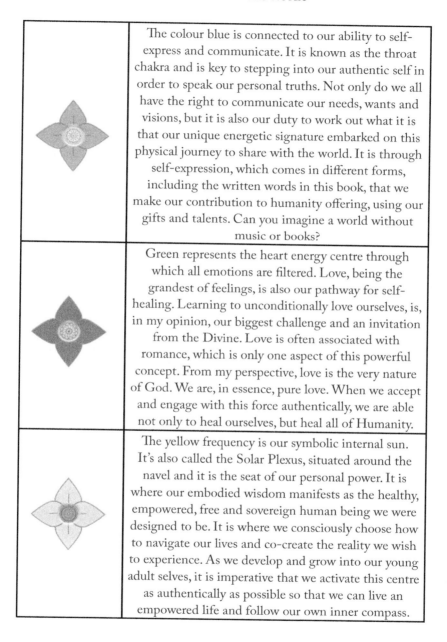

	The colour blue is connected to our ability to self-express and communicate. It is known as the throat chakra and is key to stepping into our authentic self in order to speak our personal truths. Not only do we all have the right to communicate our needs, wants and visions, but it is also our duty to work out what it is that our unique energetic signature embarked on this physical journey to share with the world. It is through self-expression, which comes in different forms, including the written words in this book, that we make our contribution to humanity offering, using our gifts and talents. Can you imagine a world without music or books?
	Green represents the heart energy centre through which all emotions are filtered. Love, being the grandest of feelings, is also our pathway for self-healing. Learning to unconditionally love ourselves, is, in my opinion, our biggest challenge and an invitation from the Divine. Love is often associated with romance, which is only one aspect of this powerful concept. From my perspective, love is the very nature of God. We are, in essence, pure love. When we accept and engage with this force authentically, we are able not only to heal ourselves, but heal all of Humanity.
	The yellow frequency is our symbolic internal sun. It's also called the Solar Plexus, situated around the navel and it is the seat of our personal power. It is where our embodied wisdom manifests as the healthy, empowered, free and sovereign human being we were designed to be. It is where we consciously choose how to navigate our lives and co-create the reality we wish to experience. As we develop and grow into our young adult selves, it is imperative that we activate this centre as authentically as possible so that we can live an empowered life and follow our own inner compass.

	The orange frequency band relates to our creativity and is connected to our sexuality. It is where our human sacred bodies are conceived and developed inside a mother's womb which, in essence, is the most sacred of our biological structures. How miraculous is it to be endowed with the ability to create and birth a human life? IDEALLY through a mutually desired and conscious conception which is agreed upon and age appropriate.
	The colour red, representing our root chakra (located at the base of our spine) has to do with safety and survival. A baby born into this human sacred body to experience life in the physical depends on her/his caregiver for all its basic needs. This is crucial for how this brand-new Divine Soul will develop, grow, and navigate life, and advance through the developmental stages activating the energy centres required to thrive. The lower energy centres are denser in frequency waves, which help us to ground and co-inhabit Planet Earth (which also has her own energy centres).

So, from the moment we are born, our energetic frequencies contained in each of our energy centres, start to develop and grow in tandem with our developmental stages.

American Psychologist Carl Rogers suggested (and I will paraphrase) that *"humans have an inner drive to self-actualise."*

I know intuitively that I am a Divine Soul in a human sacred body. However, experientially, meaning having that knowledge translated into my every action and thought, now that's a different story. Truth is, I am still embodying that awareness. The more I sit with my soul to tap into that inner knowing, the closer I get to becoming a sovereign, integral, wholesome, compassionate, benevolent, loving, empowered and **peaceful** human being.

I know in my heart who and what I am. However, there is another side to me that trips me up. My egoic mind, susceptible to external programming and societal conditioning, can work against that inner drive to self-actualise. Throughout our life's journeys, we come up against many obstacles and challenges that can take us off course. It takes courage and determination to get back on track.

My life is a demonstration of that. I have been committed to this need to self-improve and become the best version of myself despite the innerstanding that it is impossible to arrive at that state, since there will always be other levels of expansion. After all, we are infinite, and life is a dance of transformation in this never-ending game of life. Our Divine Soul's mission is to expand, express and experience life in all its colours, shapes, tastes and sounds of endless music. We can play with free will along the way, until we consciously choose what is best for the whole, when we realise we are all connected by this Divine thread and that my actions make an imprint on the tapestry of life. How would you like your piece to look and feel like?

Let's now look at the virtues a **Divine Soul** might be endowed with before I share how the soul was birthed into physical life.

Dignity: Our worth is a big part of this endeavour to embody our authentic selves. We must align with and demonstrate respect towards our own lives in order to honour who we are. What would the world be like if we all showed respect towards ourselves, each other, and the environment around us?

Integrity: It's the quality of being honest, and it's vital to our character. If we lie to ourselves and pretend everything is okay when it isn't, we compromise our integrity. Learn to be accountable to yourself and ask for assistance when you need it. I often remind my clients and mentees that asking for help is a sign of strength. Too many of us walk around living in denial.

Visionary: We are all potential visionaries. If you can use your imagination, you can think about and plan the vision for your life. An essential element, though, is doing it with wisdom. Wisdom is knowledge put into practice. If you read this book, put it on a bookshelf and forget about it, it's just data. A useful piece of information without any application becomes useless. Dare to dream your own reality, then take the actions necessary to experience it.

Influential: You are your own authority! The root cause of most problems arises when we give our power away and allow the external environment to influence and dictate our actions. We are influenced by an external world that has become tyrannical and, frankly, insane. Find your inner voice and allow your soul to influence your decisions.

Noble: When we are honest and have the courage to speak our truth and stand up for what we believe from an innerstanding point of view, and we do it with kindness and class, we show the world our nobility. The idea that a noble man or woman must belong to a particular aristocratic background is simply inaccurate. That is a construct to encourage the masses to keep their heads down and follow somebody else's rules.

Ethical: Natural Law is based on observing human nature and its intrinsic values closely. We have inherent rights and duties to respect all of life and Do No Harm. Knowing our boundaries and following our moral guidance help us conduct ourselves in a way that fosters harmony, order, honour and, ultimately, **peace.** We stand in good stead when ethics are the driving force in our actions, words, and deeds.

Sovereignty: The central point of this book is my journey from having suicidal thoughts to acknowledging the need to self-govern and to rise above both my external circumstances and the internalised traumas causing my suffering and confusion. I believe my soul had the virtue of being sovereign for me to tap into so I could become the authority of my own life and make solid, wise decisions from that stance. This is not unique to me or my soul. We are ALL sovereign beings when we choose to follow our heart's deepest desires to self-actualise. It is a personal choice and a personal responsibility to commit to the challenging paths we find along the way. I am not saying it is easy. Much to the contrary, but a choice well worth making.

Omnipotence, omniscience and omnipresence. Since our soul is a fractal of its creator source, then I believe, at our essence, we too are all-powerful, all-knowing and everywhere present. Thanks to quantum mechanics ideas, we now know that time is not linear and that our reality can simultaneously occur in the past, present, and future. We are also becoming more aware of the power and wisdom we carry within us.

Unconditional Positive Regard. I also learned from Carl Rogers that, for us to hold space for clients (and ourselves) it is vital that we observe compassion and remain non-judgmental. Human beings make mistakes all the time. I have made many and learned my lessons in the process. The Divine is not this fictional character, created by organised religion, who condemns, judges, and punishes us. We have free will (a topic for another conversation) and we must all take personal responsibility with unconditional positive regard. We can only be responsible for our own decisions whilst responding to other people's behaviours with compassion and grace (ideally). We all fall from grace but can always pick ourselves up, dust ourselves off, and get back on the path we have chosen to walk on! Our soul will be right there, cheering us on! The important thing here is to remember that our behaviour is not our true identity. We all make mistakes and it's essential that we practice unconditional positive regard to ourselves, too.

Lovingly loyal. Our soul is our best friend. She observes, holds space, respects, and has the keys to unlock all our secrets – of past lives, future lives, and the secrets to living an empowering purposeful life. Yes, it is easier said than done. Believe me, I know. It has taken me three decades to unlock my secrets. And that is why I am here with this message to inform, inspire, educate, and empower you to befriend your soul. To trust her and ask her for guidance. She is there. Always loving, always loyal, and always waiting for you to give her permission to intervene if that is what you need.

According to Austrian social reformer Rudolph Steiner – architect, occultist, esotericist, and creator of Waldorf education – the soul was **born** from the mineral kingdom. It started **feeling** through a plant; it **animated** itself in the physical sense in the animal kingdom, and it is designed to **evolve** within mankind. I read one of Steiner's books in my late teens, and felt a deep resonance with his concepts.

Imagine human life starting as a salt crystal, as life on this planet was born out of the sea. Sparks of light, i.e., Divine Souls, were infused into matter through the mineral kingdom for the first time, and our sacred human journey began. Stay with me here. It's a metaphor. Grab a pen if you don't have one already, and play with me by writing your answers down.

If you were a crystal, a rock or even a mountain, what would you be? What is it about your choice that resonates with you?

How about if you were a flower, a plant, or a tree? Close your eyes briefly and allow an image or a thought to appear. What does your soul whisper to you? How does being a species of the plant world make you feel?

What about the animal kingdom? What animal do you feel connected to? If you have any pets, do you see them having a soul like you and me?

It is unquestionable that they have feelings and know how to communicate, so there are definitely other dimensions to their lives. They also operate under the four worlds of experience, albeit in a less complex manner than humans.

Last year, my queen cat Fiora gave birth to three beautiful kittens. I was blessed to hold space for her and witness the miracle of life before my eyes. As they developed and grew into little bundles of joy, I could sense their zest for life as they explored their surroundings, played with each other, climbed trees, and had fun every single day.

This is precisely what our souls want, through the experience of having a 'body' – be it a crystal, a flower, an animal, or a human. Upon the death of the physical body and return to Spirit, I imagine there is no tangible experience anymore. I will discuss this further in a future book exploring the world of emotions.

If Steiner was right, then can you imagine the sheer intelligence you hold within you? You have the ability to be solid and steady like a mountain; the beauty and potential to blossom from a tiny seed into an exquisite sunflower; the agility and survival instinct of a cat; and finally, as a human, the transformative consciousness that drives you to be the best version of yourself to bring heaven on Earth.

We are on the brink of becoming that. We are on the verge of transforming from homo sapiens to a Universal, Cosmic Human as we activate the dormant parts of our D.N.A. I am not a scientist, and don't pretend to know how this works. What I do know, however, is that intuitively, I have no doubt that once we resolve our inner conflicts and engage with life with the reverence it deserves, we can thrive and flourish into what Source intended for us:

Divine infinite and vast intelligent nuggets of ether embodied as sovereignty itself, ornate unlimited light.

As I draw this chapter to a close, I would like to switch our attention to this idea of the Divine.

I like thinking of the Divine as holding the energetic frequency of beauty, love, grace, and gentle fierceness. It invokes in me a benevolent sense of sacredness. It also contains a subtle invitation to embark on a journey of discovery by intuitive guesswork. It signifies supernatural and magical abilities dormant within our D.N.A., just waiting to be activated.

What does the divine mean to you? What ideas resonate?

How about the idea of being eternal and infinite?

Eternity means no beginning and no end. It has always existed and will always exist. The alpha and omega of creation are in a continuum. Eternity, then, has to be infinite, limitless, and timeless, with endless possibilities.

As Divine Souls, we carry the flame of infinity on a journey of eternal creation and expression. That said, if there is no end, then it is fair to say that our soul never dies. The body perishes and returns to dust, but the unfathomable aspect of our soul, by its eternal nature, can never be extinguished.

The soul exists in a vast vacuum of possibilities traversing the multiverses beyond the edges of awareness. It dances in infinite geometries and colours, forming eternal expressions of being, visceral vitality on a never-ending journey of discoveries, doubts, and dares. Soul is a vivacious voice, vibrating the echoes of the life yet to come, and burning through the stillness of silence into the hearts of humanity.

We are that humanity. We are that vastness. We are the voices of life yet to come. The life we consciously choose to co-create when we rise to the occasion to fulfil our hearts' deepest desires. The life worth living and the life we were designed to enjoy. A life aligned and attuned to our soul and our cosmic origin.

I invite you to imagine being consciously connected to that part of you that breathes life force into your existence.

Connect with your Divine Soul!

My dear reader, when we give that inner drive Carl Rogers spoke about a chance to move towards self-actualisation, we learn to embrace who we truly are. Loving ourselves and our humanness unconditionally, we can solve all our problems.

Human beings are the unique expression of the divine Godly origin. Despite what you and I have been conditioned to believe, we are meant to be the embodiment of mother/father God incarnated as human beings. The Divine plan of Spirit is to descend upon this magnificent planet as light in the flesh. As awareness incarnated as you and me.

I Remember

I remember who I am
                    I am *awareness itself.*

I remember what I am
                    I am *awareness made flesh.*

To remember is what *I came here to do,*

So I can remember
                    WHO I came here to *BE!*

BeTalks Books © 2023 ER

I will leave you with a proverb that, for me, is a simple yet powerful reminder of who and what we truly are!

Chinese Proverb

When there is **light** in the soul, there is love in the heart.

When there is **love** in the heart, there is harmony in the home.

When **harmony** is in the home, there is order and honour in the Nation.

And when there is **order** and **honour** in the Nation, there is

Peace on Earth.

***

Dear Divine Soul,

I spent years chasing you, erroneously believing I was a human on a spiritual journey.

As I moved away from the religious doctrines I had been exposed to and began exploring my inner landscape, I realised it was the other way around.

I am a spiritual being on a physical pilgrimage, here to experience life through my sacred human body.

I am sorry it took me so long to embody that inner knowing, as everything outside of me triggered reactions that did not align with the truth of who I am.

The fear of standing out kept me captive for a long time, behaving in ways that did not line up with my true identity.

The courage it has taken me to stand in my truth, even when the whole world was telling me otherwise, has given me what no one can take away from me: my freedom of thought and my freedom of being.

For what is life without the freedom to live it as one chooses, within the parameters of Natural Law?

I no longer subscribe to fear. I no longer trust any authority outside of me.

I am my own authority. I am the author of my own life. I am not and will never be persuaded to comply with what I do not believe in.

I have transmuted suicide into sovereignty!

I am writing this book so others can do it too.

You never gave up on me, so I would not give up on myself.

Forever grateful,

Eliana

***

'We are yet to resolve our inner conflicts before establishing peace on Earth'

Written after my wake-up call at East View, April 1999

CHAPTER FOUR

Our Sacred Human Body

What We Are

Chapter 4

Our body is our Sacred Temple. It houses the spark of our Creator deep within each of us.

Life is sacred, and it is represented by the **body.**

When I held my newborn baby for the first time, I was overcome with an unconditional love which is impossible to describe. The perfection of his little hands, fingers, thumbs and nails; his little arms, legs and feet...

What a sacred moment. I felt truly blessed, and my heart overflowed.

When I think of the human body and how miraculous and perfect it is, I can't help but wonder how it is that, as our Divine Soul takes on this sacred form and breathes life into it, we lose sight of our sacredness once we are immersed into a culture and societal structures around us take over.

When I was riddled with emotional pain and felt like dying, my mind was so clouded, confused and desperate. I felt my body was a hindrance and that the only way to end my suffering was to end my life.

My journey from suicide to honouring my sovereignty was long, but it started with a decision. One cannot make such a quantum leap from one extreme state to another. It's a process. Think of it as that first step towards a thousand miles. My son called me when I was face to face with the depths of my despair, and I decided to heal rather than give in to the emotions that threatened to overwhelm me.

Emotional healing is a personal endeavour. No mainstream doctor with a pharmaceutical prescription can do that. You may find this triggering and controversial. And I am okay with that. This is my truth; as a sovereign human being, I am entitled to choose what I believe in the same way that you can choose for yourself what fits your belief system best. However, I am convinced that, had I gone down the route of antidepressants, as my GP had instructed me to do, I doubt very much I would be sitting here writing this book to tell you about my findings.

To give you context, when I walked out of my physician's office 24 years ago, I never returned and have not consulted with a doctor since. I do not subscribe to allopathic medication besides plant based and herbal remedies. I am a very healthy 61-year-old woman with plenty of energy to even teach Zumba, which is part of my holistic approach to wellness.

Now, if I break a leg or injure my physical body in a way that needs medical attention, then, of course, I would be grateful for their help. After all, they are physicians whose job is to fix the physical body. However, an illness manifest in the body has its roots in the auric fields, which I will explain further during this discourse.

And this is what I am inviting you to embark on.

I am not so naïve as to think I have all the answers by writing this short book. But what I have to tell you is worth reflecting upon.

But first, let's talk a little about the miraculous human body.

And to start this conversation, my first focus is to ask you this question:

What do you think the body needs to achieve and maintain optimal health?

I am specifically talking about the physical body and will talk you through our energetic bodies later in this chapter.

I will invite you to interact with the text again using the flower template on the following page. Like the soul flower, it is a source of **inspiration, purpose, virtues,** and **self-expression.**

Now let's explore what the body needs from us. Using the Living Flower template, write the word **body** in the middle, then pick a petal and write **nutrition.**

I'm not a nutritionist, but I know my body needs good, wholesome nutrition, so I'm mindful of what I eat and drink. I take care of my baseline by eating well-balanced foods and drinking plenty of water and other beneficial fluids.

Body Flower

We all know what is good for our bodies, and we also know what is not so good. Right? I love my food. I love eating good wholesome food, organic if possible. However, getting good quality produce you trust takes a lot of work these days.

Last year I started growing some vegetables which connected me more profoundly to the seasons, the soil, and the magic of seeds. Growing food such as tomatoes and lettuce is possible even in a small area. The gratification is precious and priceless.

Good nutrition is essential to our bodies. We, indeed, are what we consume. I say consume because it is not just about what you eat and drink. It is also about external information and the energies to which you are exposed.

Good, clean nutrition is vital to giving you the essential nutrients, vitamins, and minerals for good health. We can enjoy that pizza, wine, and chocolate as long as we take care of the baseline. It's healthy to enjoy delicious naughty stuff as well, in moderation. Isn't that what the Buddha had to teach us? The middle ground. Finding balance with everything in life is healthy and empowering for the whole of you – your body, mind, soul, and emotions.

We are here to enjoy life and taste a variety of different things. But let's make sure the essential nutrition is taken care of.

What else must we do for our bodies to maintain optimal health? Well, we need to move the body. So, on another petal, write the word: **movement.**

We use our bodies as vehicles to move our beingness around every day. Exercise is essential to build our strength and test our stamina. We can move our bodies in many ways for necessity and enjoyment. I teach Zumba, which keeps me fit and healthy in more ways than one. Find a physical activity you love and invest time and effort in doing it often. Dancing is a great way to enjoy physical exercise. Remember to be mindful of the sounds you expose yourself to, though. Remember that sound is the primal force of manifestation; its frequencies affect your vibrational energetic bodies, which can change your mental and emotional states. The music industry has become compromised and is a powerful means to lower our vibrational state.

What else do our bodies need? **Rest.** Please add the word rest to the flower template.

We need adequate sleep, and we also need to kick our shoes off and put our feet up. We must integrate movement with relaxation to allow the body to recalibrate and regulate. Sleep is also essential for our well-being. Some emotions are processed during our sleep.

Find time to sit and relax. Sit in the sun. Sit with yourself. Connect with your breath. Connect with your body. You are a human being, not a human doing. We are bombarded with distractions and so much to do as we rush around navigating life. It is essential to find time to relax.

So, nutrition, movement, and rest. What else is critical for the body? I'll add another one to complete the template but feel free to add petals to the flower and anything else you think is important to you.

We need **warmth.** We need a shelter to live in. If we are left exposed to the elements, we will struggle to survive, let alone thrive. We need protection, a blanket, and a bed to sleep on. It's essential to keep the body's temperature at a comfortable level, both in hot and cold climates. But there is another type of warmth we also need. We need each other. We need hugs. We need human contact and meaningful connections. We need to love and feel loved. Human beings need each other.

We are part of an incredible race. We just seem to have forgotten it. I believe we are in the process of discovering just how amazing and beautiful we are deep inside.

Go ahead and add more petals to the body flower with other important elements that help us achieve and maintain excellent health, such as personal hygiene, massage, cuddles, kisses and anything else your body enjoys. In addition to being efficient, our bodies are incredibly beautiful and attractive. They give us and others endless pleasure, sensation, curiosity, surprises and the ability to physically explore an infinite variety of experiences. In another word, adventure. Sometimes audacious adventure! So why would we kill it?

Let's now examine the mystical side of human design:

The human body is so magical; it is enshrouded with invisible, sacred geometrical layers the naked eye cannot see. It is so perfectly designed that it functions all by itself. All it needs from you is the fuel to power it with what it needs to work at its optimal level. I shall talk about this 'fuel' later in the chapter.

Our Sacred Human Body is so beautifully complex that it is, in fact, formed and shaped by **three main bodies:**

1. The *gross* body, the physical form, is the holographic expression of one's level of self-awareness, one's memories and what one has consumed – both in terms of nutrition and information. Your physical body is shaped in accordance with the consciousness you hold. How you think about yourself is directly related to how you treat your body and what you feed it. I am not talking about your aesthetic looks. What I am talking about is <u>fitness</u> and health, which is one of the <u>four fundamentals</u> of living as a human.

2. The *auric* body, or aura, also known as the **subtle** body, is the energetic field. It's comprised of several layers that encapsulate your gross body, and integrates all the

layers that make up 'you'. It is also called the *auric egg*, separating the individual **Divine Soul** that you are from the external world. The densest and closest to the physical body is the **etheric** body, and it holds the blueprint of your physicality; the second layer is the **emotional** field that interprets the denser, more palpable energies around you as you experience them; the third layer is the **mental** body, which processes and files your thoughts about your experiences; next is your **astral** body, responsible for expressing your thoughts and emotions as you respond to whatever is going on in your life; then there is the **etheric template** that holds the blueprint of the perfect etheric/physical body, i.e., your sacred human form. The sixth layer is the **Celestial** body, which holds the emotional and astral bodies in the higher spiritual planes. This is the layer you connect to in meditation or a state of connectedness to Source. Lastly is the **Ketheric Template**, or integrated spiritual body, meaning *crown* in Hebrew. It is the blueprint for the mental aspect of the spiritual plane. It is highly structured and holds the information you need for your current lifetime brought forth from previous ones. Now, you may or may not believe in past lives, and that is perfectly okay, but it does not alter its validity and the fact that it is a vital part of your makeup.

3. The *causal* body is the seed for your Divine Soul that causes the body to be made manifest as matter, carrying your lifetimes of lessons, experiences and karmic baggage. In that sense, it is the home for your soul to return to when it matures and reaches the appropriate time for it to lose its body 'shell' and transition to the spiritual world from whence it came.

In my pursuit to discover who and what I truly am, I started putting these pieces together to assist me in navigating my life. As I found some answers and discerned between what resonated with me as truth and what didn't, I couldn't help but ask myself: *'How come I didn't learn any of this in my Biology class?'*

Why are schools and other societal systems so negligent in giving us essential information and tools to help us live a sovereign and empowered life?

Well, my dear reader, I figured out the answer for myself and would invite you to contemplate these questions, too. There is a vast sea of information about this in published books and on the Internet. Please do your own research, as the above is only the tip of the iceberg. You will find some links in the reference section of this book to get you started.

However, it's essential to discern what feels true for you because this 'sea' is compromised with toxic, false, and misleading information, so one must sort through to find the pearls of wisdom hidden within the mysteries of life. Trust your soul. She will know what is true.

For now, let's continue to uncover and acknowledge the miraculous sacredness of our physicality.

The human body is so intelligent that it has **three** brains!

The head brain, the heart brain and the gut brain:

1. The **cephalic** brain (head brain) is divided into three and is responsible for cognition, perception, and language acquisition. It allows us to process and exchange information.

The **reptilian** (primal) brain is the oldest and is the seat of the unconscious mind; the **paleomammalian** (chemical) brain regulates our internal chemistry. It is responsible for the limbic system, a set of brains structures that supports functions such as emotions, behaviour, long-term memory and the sense of smell.

The **neomammalian** (rational) brain, also known as the neocortex, is the most evolved and specialised brain. It helps us to think and solve problems.

2. The **cardiac** brain (heart brain) is responsible for sending emotional signals to the body as a whole and is connected to what you value in life and how you feel about your experiences.

3. The **enteric** brain (gut-brain) regulates our hormones, metabolism, and blood pressure and helps us process information during sleep. According to an article from The Sangha House's Centre for Health and Wellbeing, almost 95% of serotonin, the happy hormone, is found in the gut. All three brains work together to create your life experiences through the body, and each body-brain can learn, change and communicate.

I am not a neuroscientist; the above is simplistic information for a highly complex subject. But like the **three main bodies**, it serves as context to illustrate our amazing body's intelligence, power, richness, and magic.

And to affirm this magic and illustrate the Divine's presence within the fabric of our humanness, here is what I found out about our DNA when Spirit whispered to me during a powerful plant medicine retreat:

The human body is NOT meant to hold trauma.

The body is meant to acclimate, hold LIGHT, and shine like a diamond. If everything is energy vibrating as frequency, when we see the stars shining in the sky, it is their light, i.e., the energy field emanating from their life force in the cosmic realm. Well, we are made of the same life force energy, birthed from God's desire to Be. Remember Steiner's claim that a soul is born in the crystal; therefore, we are becoming crystalline in our structure as we unravel the mysteries of our DNA. We now know that our DNA has a massive percentage of untapped potential. Why is that? Recently, I have learned the literal meaning of DNA as follows:

Deoxy- (from Latin means God) ribbon (Rabbi)

Nucleic = at the centre

Acid = alchemical fire

In other words, **DNA means that God is the fire at the centre of our being.** So biologically speaking, we have God in our genetic makeup. Prime Creator is at the very centre of our bodies. The God molecule is the blueprint to make a human being. But Who or What is this primordial source of creation? The Bible states, *'In the beginning was the word, and the **word** was God. The word **became flesh** and dwelled amongst men.'*

This is exciting news, and I invite you to pause here momentarily.

Breathe this in:

God is at the centre of your being.

It is the fire in your belly.

All elements exist inside us and are represented in our makeup. Our sacred human bodies carry Mother Earth's natural ingredients within them. That's powerful information.

Water as your blood

Air, your breath

Earth, your bones

Fire your soul.

We have sacred medicine within us. Our bodies are so efficient and wise that they can produce their inner healing pharmacy by conscious breath work alone!

My breathwork and alchemist mentor Christopher August reminds us of who and what we are by stating the following during his fire element breathwork on his powerful album Soul Rise:

"You are a Divine spark of the creative life force energy, and as you connect with your power within, this golden LIGHT, channelling through you like a beacon of energy, transmitting a higher frequency of vibration into your auric field, illuminates the Spirit within."

This powerful information!

Now let me share a session I had with a young person contemplating suicide. I was working as a school-based

Counsellor at the time, and the recreated session below has been based on her story. This book is truly all about the technique I used to inform, inspire, educate, and empower her to make an informed decision. I wish for you to take on board its teachings, adapt them, make them your own, and use them when relevant and appropriate. This is my gift to you, and I trust you will show the respect and sensitivity required for this sacred work.

Eliana (the students call me Ellie):

Hi Jaz. Come on in. Take a seat. As usual, let's pause briefly. Take a moment to leave everything behind that door as you walk in. Whatever class you came out of, anything that has been in your mind. Put everything in an imagined box and leave it outside for now. It's safe in the box, and you can bring it in here if you feel it is appropriate and relevant for today's session.

Take a breath. Ahh…

If you feel comfortable, close your eyes, and allow your emotions to settle. Have a sense of your heartbeat, the temperature in the room, the sound of my voice, the noises going on outside.

Another deep breath and relax into the chair if you can. Open your eyes, and welcome to your seventh session. You are getting used to me now, right? Or do you still find it weird?

Jaz

Yeah, I quite like it now, Ellie. I have to confess I look forward to it.

Ellie

Okay, well, first things first. I'd like to say thank you. Thank you for showing up. Thank you for honouring your word.

The last session was quite a challenging one for both of us, wasn't it?

Jaz

Uh huh.

Ellie

It was intense but was needed. Thank you for your courage to open up. This is a very delicate and complex subject to talk about. I am humbled and honoured that you shared your feelings with me.

Jaz

Yes. I felt I could trust you, Ellie.

Ellie

So I'd like to acknowledge you for trusting me and discussing your feelings about your intention to end your life. Did you have any of those thoughts since then?

Jaz

Yes, I did, but I managed to do what you suggested and distracted myself. I went for a run and listened to my music. I also avoided staying in my room alone. Thank you for all that you have done for me, Ellie. I still feel like I can't cope, but seeing you does help. You are different from anyone I have spoken to before. It feels like you really listen to me.

Ellie

That's what I am here for, Jaz. I am glad you feel heard. And it makes all the difference if you feel you can talk to me openly. When you circled 'self-harm' on our initial assessment and the information on your referral notes, I knew I needed to ensure you felt seen, heard and held. We talked about self-harm and how it comes in many guises. Do you remember?

Jaz

Uh huh.

Ellie

I honour you for opening up and discussing your intentions of committing suicide. You knew I would have to act by sharing that information with the school's safeguarding officer to keep you safe, so I am happy to see you here. I thought about you often and was eager to see you today.

Are you okay with us picking up from where we left off and working on this?

Jaz

I think so. What can you do, Ellie?

Ellie

My job is to inform, inspire, educate, and empower you emotionally and help you make good decisions about your life.

It's a process, though. There is no magic, but I can help you if you allow me to. I'd like to acknowledge you because I told you I had something specific and helpful to share, so now that you are here, let's take another breath before I share an activity with you. Is there anything you need to say or ask?

Jaz

No, not really, Ellie, but I just want this pain to end and these thoughts to leave me alone. I'm still feeling down. (Jaz starts crying).

Ellie

You are safe here, Jaz.

Let it all out. I know it's complicated, and I know it isn't fair.

Is there anything, in particular, you would like to talk about right now?

Jaz

I don't think so, Ellie. I just want to be happy. I hate school; everything is so messed up. I can't cope with the pressure. All the exams and all the expectations. I just want to run away from it all.

Ellie

You are stronger than you think, Jaz. I promise you. Life is unpredictable and mostly unfair, but what matters is not what happens to us but what we do about what happens. It becomes much easier when we have the relevant information and the tools. When we know better, we can do better and become better at living an empowered and joyful life. We have touched on awareness and how knowledge is power. Yeah? Today, I will give you some information that may change your perspective. Shall I do that?

Jaz

Yes, please.

Ellie

Okay, so last week, after you categorically told me you were planning to take your own life, I felt it was appropriate to share with you that my husband committed suicide, and that is the reason why I am here today, working as a counsellor to inform individuals like yourself who are experiencing this agonising predicament. I've been there, too, Jaz. I appreciate how vulnerable we can feel. But here I am. I have come to the other end. And I have gifts which I'd like to offer you.

Shall we go for it? Would you like me to share this gift with you?

Jaz

Yes, yes, of course. I trust you, Ellie. You're different. You're not like my teachers or most adults I know. Being with you makes me feel calm. And I feel safe. So thank you for being so patient and so, I don't know, you are just different, and I like coming here. I really do.

Ellie

It means a lot to hear you say that, Jaz. It really does. And I know you are here because you chose to be here, not because you were told to. I know you were initially reluctant and suspicious, but you came back, so well done!

Okay, are you ready?

Jaz

Yes!

Ellie

Cool. So tell me, Jaz, does the name Aristotle mean anything to you?

Jaz

Was he a Greek dude?

Ellie

He was a Greek philosopher who said, "The whole is greater than the sum of all its parts." I'll say that again.

"The whole is bigger or greater than the sum of all its parts."

That's an existential idea. Do you know what I mean by that?

Jaz

Not sure.

Ellie

Well, it refers to matters concerning the meaning of life and that type of thing. It's about contemplating and exploring life as humans as we exist in this space and time. Let's explore what Aristotle might have meant about that statement. And I've created a metaphor using a four-petalled flower to explain that. But before I do, I'm interested; what would you be if you were a flower?

Jaz

Mmm, I like daffodils. Yeah, I would be a daffodil. They make me happy when they appear all over the place in springtime.

Ellie

Lovely. I love daffodils, too.

Okay, so let's think of a flower. A flower has petals, a stem, leaves, and the middle bit called a pistil. And roots. Each part combined makes up the physical form of a certain flower, like a daffodil, for example. But there is more to the flower than the sum of all its parts. There is a metaphysical or unseen aspect as well. There is an essence to a flower. There is beauty to a flower. There is perfume to a flower, so Aristotle's idea about the whole being greater than adding all its physical parts together relates to this metaphysical facet of whatever we might be talking about.

Even this conversation we are having right now. There is so much more to engaging in a counselling intervention than meeting once a week. If it is done sensitively and mindfully from both sides, then a thread continues to tie this therapeutic conversation together until we meet again.

Does that make sense to you, Jaz? What is going on for you right now?

Jaz

Yeah, that makes a lot of sense. Thank you, Ellie.

Ellie

Okay, so let's do an activity together. I am going to show you my Life Flower. Are you okay with that?

Jaz

Sure.

Ellie

Great!

What I have here is a template of a four-petalled flower. What's your favourite colour, Jaz?

Jaz

I like yellow.

Ellie

Okay, cool. I love yellow too. I like bright colours. You can tell by the clothes I wear, right?

I will lightly shade the flower's centre yellow and then write your name. Okay, I will give you the template and guide you through completing the activity. Is that okay?

Jaz

Yep.

Ellie

Fabulous! You can see some coloured pencils on my little table, yeah? Please take a red pencil and on the petal facing down or south, please lightly shade it in red and write the word: **Body**.

Let's use the four directions to carry on. Once you finished with the 'body' petal, please take a blue pencil and do the same process and this time, pick the petal facing west, as in the compass, shade it and write the word: **Mind**.

When you are ready, choose the purple pencil and on the north petal, I'd like you to write: **Soul**.

So now we have the east petal left, and when you are done with the soul petal, using a green pencil, please write the word: **Emotions.**

So existentially speaking, you know that quote from Aristotle? It is an existential quote that invites us to think about the meaning of life. Questions like 'Who am I and what am I doing here' are existential ideas. Are you with me?

Jaz

Yeah, I think so, Ellie. I sometimes wonder what this shit life is all about.

Ellie

Those questions are really important for us to ask and answer for ourselves. No one has your answers. We can learn all sorts of stuff by going to school and engaging with our communities and cultures, but existential questions are for the individual to contemplate. Of course, there are guidelines, and ideally, what I am going to share with you will assist you in making sense of it in a way that works for you. Is it okay for me to continue?

Jaz

Yes, I'm really curious now.

Ellie

Awesome!

So, existentially speaking, we operate on four different levels.

We have a body, but that's not who we are. It's part of what we are, in a sense. Life is represented by the body, so it is our skin, flesh, and bones suit, if you like. We are not our bodies, and the body will eventually perish and die. Ideally through natural causes, so it can return to Source in the spiritual world.

We have bodies to navigate life with.

We also have a mind, and we use the mind to learn, think, reflect and create our experiences. The mind is far more complex than that, but for the purpose of today, let's just say we create the life we wish to live, using the mind when we make decisions and then take action. Are you following me so far?

Jaz

Yeah, that's really interesting, Ellie

Ellie

Cool. I'm glad you think so, Jaz. You can take the template with you when we finish if you like.

Jaz

Yes, please. I'd like to take it.

Ellie

Right, so let's take a look at the soul petal. This is the spiritual element of human beings. Even if you don't believe in that kind of thing, such as the spiritual world, it's okay. Just bear with me for a moment.

By the way, I am not asking you to believe in everything I am saying. It's for you to reflect on and come to your own conclusions. And that goes for everything in life, Jaz. You don't have to take on board what others tell you. We all have the right to speak our truths and allow others to speak theirs. You need to reflect and discern. See how it makes you feel and if it makes sense for you to believe it or not. Would you agree?

Jaz

Definitely. But I don't feel anyone listens to me. Well, apart from you. It's like I have no voice. This is why I feel so depressed. I don't know how to speak up and ask for what I want. I just do as I'm told and stay quiet. But inside, I'm like screaming. And that's why I feel so depressed, I think. I feel so sad at home and stressed at school. And that's why I want to die. I can't see the point, you know?

Ellie

I do, Jaz. I really do. I get it. I was fifteen once, and I resonate with what you are saying. You are still young and finding your way through life. It will come with your experiences, but you must be given appropriate and relevant guidance along the way. That's what I am here for, Jaz. I can guide you along the way if you choose to. I can show you the way, but you are the one who needs to walk it. Does that make sense?

Jaz

Yeah, it does, but it all seems so hard.

Ellie

I know it does, Jaz. However, it is all relative, and everything can be viewed from different perspectives. You are far more powerful than you realise, and I am here to remind you of that and give you some tips on how to tap into that inner power.

Depression is the lack of self-expression! It's no wonder you feel depressed. You just said you feel like you have no voice. When we suppress our feelings, wants and needs, we struggle to feel aligned with our true essence.

It's all about self-awareness and emotional intelligence. The more you know about the truth of who you are, the more you can see that life is not what happens to you but how you deal with the stuff that happens. And you don't have to do it solo. Asking for help is a sign of strength, so please don't ever suffer quietly by yourself. That's where the danger is. Okay? I am here for you, Jaz, and there will be plenty of other helping hands as you grow up. Please look for help whenever you need it. For now, let's get back to the last petal.

Emotions are one of the four existential levels. So we have the body, mind, soul, and emotions. And this is where we usually get stuck.

Emotions are energy in motion, so they need to be felt. In a sense, emotions become our superpower when we know how to experience and deal with them. Emotions either give us pleasure or pain. The emotions themselves are not, in a sense, good or bad for us. They are neutral from the perspective of 'experience'. The meaning we give them gives us the feelings that arise from them.

The problem is when we don't allow them to arise or to be felt and suppress them instead.

We are spiritual beings on a human journey, and the very purpose of this journey is so that we experience it. Right? As far as I innerstand, our Spirit cannot feel without a physical body, so we need a body to embark on this game we call life. If we see it as a game, it motivates us to play it. Similar to a video game, there are obstacles and challenges along the way so we can overcome and reach higher levels and more adventures to embark on.

Does that make 'life' more attractive? If you see it as a game you chose to play? You must deal with the obstacles as you get better at playing it. As you learn to solve your problems, you get stronger and therefore more empowered to make good decisions and create a life you truly wish to experience. It is how we perceive life that really matters.

If the school feels stressful, I suggest asking yourself, 'What can I do about it?' You can learn to manage stress. Then take the necessary actions. It is easier said than done, but it is possible, so let's focus on that rather than allowing the emotions to overwhelm you. I have a formula to share for managing emotions, but we won't have time to go through that today. The purpose of today is for you to realise that suicide is not a wise move. And it will become clear in just a moment. Are you okay for me to continue?

Jaz

Yes, I'm intrigued.

Ellie

Fantastic! You are doing great, Jaz. And I'm right here.

So looking at the Living Flower template we have completed, let's imagine we pluck the body petal out of it. Yeah? Let me cover it up and pretend it is no longer there.

Jaz

Okay.

Ellie

My question is, has the flower ceased to exist?

Jaz

Well, no. It's still got the three other petals and the centre.

Ellie

Exactly!

What if I told you that the same applies to human beings?

Jaz

What do you mean?

Ellie

Do you remember I said we have a body but are not our bodies?

Jaz

Yes.

Ellie

Let's say that this four-petal flower represents a human being. So the centre of the flower is the idea of the self. Think of the self as the whole, which Aristotle was referring to. We exist and operate on all these four levels of experience, and when the body dies, the other three aspects of who we are, don't. These are the metaphysical sides of our beings, so if it's not physical but exists, then it can't die. Even if you don't believe in having a soul or a spiritual dimension, you can't deny that you have a mind and experience your emotions. Are you with me?

Jaz

I guess so. It makes sense, Ellie.

Ellie

This is profound stuff to think about, but it's relevant to what we are dealing with here, Jaz. The truth of the matter is when your body dies, the invisible parts of you have to go somewhere. It goes to the invisible plane it came from. I believe it goes back to Source. It returns home. Tell me, Jaz. What is it about suicide that attracts you?

Jaz

I just want my pain to go away. I hate my life!

Ellie

So this idea of suicide, let's explore this because it's really important that you get where I'm going with this, okay? Are you up for that?

Jaz

Yes!

Ellie

Look at this four-petal flower. Let's say it represents a human life. However, if we eliminate the red petal that represents the body, we are left with the mind, the soul and the emotions, agreed?

Jaz

Yes.

Ellie

And these aspects of ourselves return to another dimension – let's call it a spiritual dimension – where the mind and the emotions can be integrated. So technically, these two elements carry the essence of your experiences. They are then integrated into the soul or the metaphysical side of you and don't die.

Now there is an important distinction that we need to make because natural death and deliberate death, such as suicide, will impact how these invisible aspects are fused upon death.

Would it be fair to say that the depression, sadness, stress, and any other emotion you are experiencing is not a bodily sensation but an emotional-mental distress?

Jaz

Yes, it's not really physical. It's more in my head and how I feel, but not a pain in my body.

Ellie

Exactly. Perfectly said Jaz. That is exactly right. Although the suffering you are experiencing is processed through the body, it is not located in the body like a toothache or a stomach ache, right?

Jaz

Yes.

Ellie

Okay, so I'm going to ask you a very important question. Are you ready?

Jaz

I think so.

Ellie

And remember, you don't have to agree with me. I am giving you some food for thought, and I invite you to reflect on it and see how it makes you feel.

Can I continue?

Jaz

Yes.

Ellie

If the pain is not in the body, it is stored in your mental-emotional aspect, so my question is: What do you think might happen to the pain when your body dies? Do you think the pain will cease to exist? Think about the petals of my metaphorical flower we've been working on.

Jaz

If we compare it to the flower petals, the pain won't stop if I kill myself. Is that what you are saying, Ellie?

Ellie

I'm afraid so, Jaz. That is what I believe, as there is no guarantee your suffering will end by eliminating the body. You are a Divine Soul that is eternal and infinite at your core.

You are a beautiful soul and have your whole life ahead of you, Jaz. Suicide is a permanent action. You cannot undo it whilst your emotions are temporary. You are feeling overwhelmed with doubts, sadness and confusion at the moment, but they will pass. Once you learn to embrace and work through your emotions, you will find your inner power and fight instead of wanting to take flight.

I am not saying it is easy, Jaz. But I am saying it is possible, and I have faith in you. You can do this. I can help you.

After a brief pause, Jaz looks at me and says:

Jaz

I have never thought about it this way…

But what can I do about it then? I want this pain to stop!

Ellie

Well, I can't prove any of this. I just know it, deep, deep down. Like you, I had suicidal thoughts at the lowest point in my life. I also thought about it when I was about your age, as I felt I didn't fit in and the world around me didn't make sense. I was scared of those thoughts, but they returned when I was 37. My husband, Roger, killed himself when he was 38. I didn't know any of this at that time, so I couldn't help him. But I know it today so I can help you.

You can kill your body but can't kill that spark of who you are and where you came from.

I'm mindful of the time and must ensure you leave my room with a better plan.

You asked me what you can do about it, and here's my answer.

Jaz's eyes are wide open, and she looks as if she is entirely wrapped up at the moment, waiting for what I am going to say next.

My good friend, Marcus West, once said:

"The only way to it is the way through it."

Whatever life throws at us, the most effective and empowering way for us to deal with it is head-on. We can't run away from life. We can't hide or suppress our emotions. They need to be felt and processed so we can move on and learn from our experiences. It's what we are here for. To experience our lives, not to give it up. If you suppress your emotions, they will get stuck in your energetic field – your subtle body – and if unresolved, emotions will manifest as a physical illness sooner or later.

Life is sacred, so your body is sacred!

Jaz, we are coming to the end of our session, and I know you have a class to attend. I need to make sure you are feeling up to it. Tell me how you are feeling right now. Does any of this make sense to you? I would like your word that you will reflect on this. You can journal about it. Talk to someone you trust. Promise me you will return next week for us to continue this work.

You see, there is no magic and no quick fixes. The only way is to do the inner work required to overcome your emotions and find the dormant power within you. So, how are you feeling, Jaz?

Jaz

I am feeling quite uplifted, actually, Ellie. I really am. I had never thought about these things, but it makes sense. I feel like a cloud has lifted, and I feel with your help, I can do this. Thank you so much, Ellie.

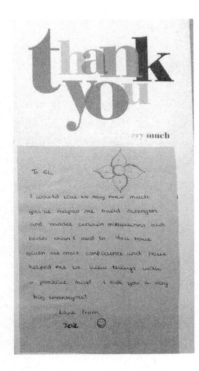

Ellie

The journey of a thousand miles begins with the first step, Jaz. That step is the decision we make. What are you choosing, Jaz? What is your decision?

Jaz

I want to live, Ellie. I want to be able to deal with my problems, and I want to be happy.

Ellie

Well, then, let's make your next appointment. With your permission, I will inform the pastoral officer that I am extending your sessions for another series of eight appointments to ensure I give you the tools you need. I am not saying I have a magic wand, and all your problems will disappear. Living an empowered life means you can rise above your circumstances, knowing you are more powerful and stronger than the challenges you face.

Same day and time next week?

Jaz

Yes, please, Ellie. I look forward to seeing you. Thank you so much!

The Living Flower

I have no doubt we are powerful beyond measure. Divine Souls having a human journey in a sacred human form means we are meant to evolve and thrive.

So why is it that we are seeing the worst playing out among us?

Why are we killing ourselves?

Why are we killing each other?

Why is humanity so entangled in pain and suffering?

When I think of Roger's tragic and untimely death, along with millions (if not billions) of other souls who committed suicide because they didn't remember in time how magnificent and powerful they were, I get even more compelled to bring this information out so you can remember and help others in your circle to remember, too.

I believe in the power of self-awareness and emotional intelligence to help us transcend, transmute, and transform the tragedies, traumas, and tears into valuable lessons for us to evolve and thrive.

This is the most important piece in the whole of this book.

This is where I circle back to that dreadful Sunday. That night the police knocked on my door.

The day Roger hanged himself on the cherry tree in our back garden.

This is the piece I get to talk you through, the most crucial part of this book.

What is behind the act of committing suicide?

Where did the idea come from?

When?

How?

And why?

When I was in my teens and thought about dying, the attraction was the possibility that I would return home, where I really belonged, and reunite with the source of light I came from: The Divine Mother Father God that created my soul.

However, I remember feeling scared of those thoughts, as a stronger voice told me those thoughts weren't mine. A part of me knew I had a covenant and a code to follow. Deep down, I knew I could never die anyway, but if I killed my body, my soul could be damaged in the process. I didn't have the language to articulate that when I was 14, but it is a knowing I have come to uncover from my own depths as life guided me here, writing this book, to share the truth I have come to know.

Please take a breath here.

Let's pause for a moment.

What I have to say may be triggering and controversial. I realise that. However, it is my truth, and I must express it. It is my soul's mission to self-express. Remember the soul flower? My soul has inspired me to follow my purpose and be guided by my virtues to share my unique light as a message to humanity.

So here it goes. Are you ready?

The truth about suicide is this:

Suicide is an idea inserted into the human psyche and infiltrated into our lives through literature, films, television, radio, and other mediums. It found its way into our minds, homes, relationships, and cultures to plague humanity with its spells.

Let's think of Romeo and Juliet for a moment. What a powerful film. I remember watching it as a young person. I didn't know what to make of it at the time, so I brushed it aside. It's called art and 'entertainment'. We go to the cinema for entertainment, right? We read books to learn and inform ourselves and escape our own realities and get a glimpse of someone else's worldview. Like you are doing right now.

So, I ask you, do you think ideas can creep into your mind and take hold there as a thought form?

With the suicide rate at its peak all over the world, I believe there is an even more sinister aspect to it. It has become an epidemic. It is heartbreaking to know that the number of individuals taking their own lives is increasing. I have to do whatever it takes to make sure people are making an informed decision. I can't stop anyone from committing this act, but I can share this message far and wide to tell you that **killing your body does not guarantee the end of your suffering.**

In Goethe's 1774 novel, The Sorrows of Young Werther, a young man puts a gun to his head to end his agony of unrequited love. It became known as the Werther effect, and prompted young European men to dress like Werther and take their lives. It is also called Contagion Effect, or copycat suicide. As one person does it, it makes it **permissible** for others to do it, too.

While undertaking my counselling degree at the then University of Glamorgan in 2007 and 2008, at least 26 young people committed suicide in the Bridgend County Borough in South Wales. I was stunned with horror. When I heard that the Welsh Government would pass a law to make counselling compulsory in Welsh Schools, I knew exactly where I was headed with my new career. And having worked with clients like Jaz, I feel humbled and honoured to have been able to inform her in time.

So, if suicide is an idea propagated as an 'art form' and subliminally encouraged throughout history, then there is another word I must use to dispel this dreadful, agonising epidemic.

Our mind-brain is like computer software. I don't have the space in this short book to talk about the human mind, but bear with me for a moment as I point you in the direction I am going with this message.

Computer software is a set of instructions or programs that executes specific tasks. If our minds are like software, then they're programmable, right? There are obvious advantages to using our minds to operate routine tasks without much effort. Over time, tasks like brushing our teeth become second nature, and we don't even have to think about it. It's the thing we do in the mornings and before we go to bed. Our minds are impressionable, and we are exposed to endless pieces of information every single day via television, radio, the Internet, and social media. The sounds and visions we are exposed to subliminally influence our thoughts, so I invite you to be mindful of the information you consume.

We are currently experiencing a tidal wave of misinformation and disinformation. We have been misled and manipulated. So here it goes, my dear reader. Are you ready for this? There is no other way to say this, but go ahead and say it! Suicide is a program that has been running in the background, subliminally at first, but has now reached a point we can no longer deny.

I cannot, and do not, accept that a Divine Soul, with a mission to evolve and a drive to self-actualise, would choose to incarnate in a sacred human body only to extinguish its light. It doesn't make sense. The only explanation I find reasonable is that something more nefarious is at play here.

We just have to look at the world right now. It is 2023, and humanity is divided, with a massive percentage of people living in intense fear, dread, suffering, anxiety, trauma, and so on. **Why is that?**

If we are a Divine Soul in a sacred human body, why is it that we are not living a life that translates our inner state of peace, love, benevolence, compassion, and joy?

Well, in case you haven't noticed or have been blinded by cognitive dissonance, there is a spiritual war going on. There are many facets to this war, but ultimately, is it a war to conquer your soul, the human soul. And it has been going on for a very long time.

The most detrimental and terrifying thought about suicide is that not only is the sacred human body being deliberately exterminated, but it is highly possible that your soul will be damaged in the process. And this is a very scary thought.

Let me bring you back to the causal body or the perfect spiritual blueprint for the entire history of your soul's journey across time and space. What could happen if that blueprint is compromised? Is damaging your soul the ultimate goal of the evil forces that have been running and ruining this beautiful planet?

This is a deep and complex question.

We don't even know how powerful we are. This book is about my journey from suicide to sovereignty. Lying on the floor ready to take a handful of pills, my mind had been taken over. I was cut off from my true essence. I was cut off from my heart-brain, unable to hear it. So Divine intervention came to my rescue in the form of my child's voice, calling out for me.

My dear reader, suicide is a corrupt idea that became a program. It is a thought form – one that can infiltrate our minds from the field of information all around us, encouraging us to self-execute. Just like a computer virus, it must be deleted.

Why is that? Well, this is a complex issue and a topic to explore in another conversation. We have been granted free will, and if we are honest, we have made a mess of it. We are all responsible. Even to the extent we didn't know we were being misled.

To paraphrase Sartre, we are cursed with freedom and have come to a point in our evolution when it is time for us to choose more consciously. I am no longer prepared to compromise my choices, and this invites you to think carefully about yours.

Roger made his choice so I could live to tell the tale. I am not willing to allow his tragic death to be in vain. I am truly sorry I was not in the position to hold space for him, as my son did for me. But perhaps we engaged in a soul contract so that I could be sharing this message as a warning to humanity and an invitation to open our eyes and see more clearly.

Roger did what he did, and I was there to pick up the pieces. I've spent the past 33 years doing just that: putting those pieces together. I focused on embodying my sovereignty, and deleted the suicide program.

We are creator beings. We are powerful beings. With relevant, inspiring information and an empowering set of tools, together we can achieve what we came here to achieve. By acknowledging and honouring who and what we truly are, we can expand our consciousness and activate that inner drive to evolve and thrive in joy.

We can live longer, healthier, more wholesome and beautiful lives in communion with each other. We can offer cooperation and respect. Inspired by our Divine Soul, we can follow our purpose, tap into our guidance, and articulate it. We can express our uniqueness as true artists, and create a world where we wish to belong. For that, we must change our course and embrace our sovereignty.

Let us all live from our sovereign inner state – the place of true power. I made my decision. I am the author of my own life. I am my own authority. And you, my reader, can tap into that, too, if that's what you choose. Go spread this information, and live it for yourself.

You are a spark of the Creator Source. Own it and let it shine through your amazing sacred human form.

I'm a **solutionary!**

I am here to give solutions. The only way to it is the way through it.

I am not saying it is easy. We are all riddled with traumas. We must resolve them, one by one. They don't belong in our bodies. Our bodies are meant to carry light. Light is awareness made flesh. Here are some suggestions:

- Find spiritual practices that resonate with you, so you can nourish your soul.

- Learn to efficiently manage your emotions and turn them into your superpower.

- Take care of your sacred human body. Honour and respect your life.

- Speak your truth. Self-expression is part of your soul's mission as it evolves throughout time and space. Find what you are passionate about and make your passion your profession.

***

My dear reader,

As I bring this chapter and the message in this book to a close, I trust that you have benefited from reading this text in more ways than one. It is my truth, and I know many will not accept it as theirs.

However, should it resonate with you, I sincerely wish that you use this information as a magical power to assist humanity during these difficult yet transformative times.

I invite you to focus on solutions and finding joy in life's simple but meaningful aspects. Sit with your soul often. Listen to her whispers and follow her guidance. She is always there. You will never be alone.

Stop consuming fear-based information. It doesn't serve you. Pursue your passions. Allow your soul to lead you to the sacredness of your being. You are beautiful. You are powerful. You are magical. You are the loving radiant seed of Divine potential that we can't comprehend with our human minds. However, we can sense it with our inner peace, power, wisdom and awareness.

Give yourself permission to trust and love yourself unconditionally. We could solve all the problems in the whole world by learning to love ourselves.

Peace is an inside job.

Power is a conscious choice.

Wisdom is knowledge in action, and

Awareness is light made flesh, as your Divine Soul in your Sacred human body.

Let's remember who and what we truly are, so we can be the magic and medicine the world needs during these transitional times in our human her-story.

Deep gratitude,

Eliana Regina

www.betalksbooks.com

Mountains

As the mountains, I stand tall
Listening to the silent whisper reminding
They are my only walls...

With the mountains, I sit still
Waiting for ancient wisdom
The winds have distilled.

In her core, a mountain births her kingdoms
In a stormy marriage
To the oceans that conceived her.

At her summit, in awe, I fall deep
Travelling thus far,
In pursuit of whom I seek.

By her feet, she gathers her offsprings.
As we walk through eternity,
Playing the role of a thousand Kings.

Beyond the shores of her waters,
She displays beauty and glory
Witnessing humanity unfold their story.

The rivers and lakes adorn you
In a perfect and seamless robe
Blessed I am to walk with you around the globe.

As sacred as a mountain top,
Crowned by pure white light,
I hereby declare who I am through my insights.

I have a message to give
As awareness fills my heart,
In remembrance of what I've come here to impart.

As majestic as a snowy mountain,
We, too, play a royal part
By claiming our sovereignty and sharing our art.

Like the mountains, we have crystals in our bones;
Cosmic waters run through us as we breathe our liberty
Stoking the Spiritual Fire of Divinity.

As a mountain, I, too, am strong.
There is power in my presence,
Bringing forth my unique song.

All of the above is truly just to say,
We are Divine in our nature
And Sacred in many ways...

Divine Soul, Sacred Body

EPILOGUE

A Way Forward

Divine Soul, Sacred Body

Epilogue

So, if *'we are divine sparks of a Creator God, in a sacred human body',* why are we killing ourselves, killing each other and causing such devastation on Planet Earth?

These questions fuelled my attempt to answer at least one of them:

WHY ARE WE KILLING OURSELVES?

Why would a Benevolent, Loving and Almighty God create such a beautiful and bounty planet, all the living species to inhabit it, infuse it with an eternal, infinite and cosmic spark of light that propels us forth to evolve and thrive, only to allow us to extinguish it?

When my husband committed suicide, it made no sense to me. When I started suffering from depression and contemplated doing the same, God intervened and asked me another set of questions.

Those questions led me to write this book, which I have resisted for a very long time. I worked through the resistance, and this book became my life's purpose. My north and my guiding star. It took on a life of its own, becoming more significant than my pathetic doubts about myself.

Now that you have read my material, I invite you to process its information in whatever manner works for you, so it can enrich your awareness about these existential questions.

During the course of writing this manuscript, it became clear that I couldn't stop here, so this is my opportunity to tell you about the upcoming sequel, called **Creative Mind, Empowering Emotions.** It's already in the works, and I will do my very best to get it published as soon as possible as a way forward from learning the truth about who and what we are:

A Divine Soul in a Sacred Human Body, here on this magnificent physical planet to experience the game called LIFE. Go live it, with all its trials and tribulations. Celebrate the highs and honour the lows, as it is in the lowlands that we gather ourselves up, take a breath, and jump right back on the rollercoaster for the thrills only life in a physical form can provide.

Deep gratitude,

Eliana

About the Author

Eliana is a specialist in self-awareness and emotional literacy. She received her undergraduate degree in Counselling from the University of South Wales (formerly known as the University of Glamorgan). She worked as a School-based Counsellor and in 2012, published *A Book About Us: Celebrating Diversity* with a view to offering emotional intelligence workshops for school-aged children and young people.

Eliana co-authored *The Everyday Girl's Guide to Living in Truth, Self-Love and Acceptance*, published by Balboa Press, and is the co-author of the best-selling book *She Speaks Her Truth: Women's Words Changing the World.*

Originally from Brazil, Eliana emigrated to Wales after marrying her Welsh Prince Charming, Roger John, in 1989. The following year, Roger committed suicide. For the past 33 years, Eliana has been on a journey of self-enquiry and has invested vastly in her quest for self-actualisation. She feels that counselling and general talk therapies are not empowering enough. *"People are emotionally battered and spiritually starved,"* she says. *"Humanity needs better tools to tap into inner power and resilience."*

Eliana has written this book aiming to inform, inspire, educate, and empower college and university students across the globe in general, but particularly those training in counselling and other human sciences. Professionals in the field and any open-minded individual can also benefit from reading her work.

At age 61, Eliana teaches Zumba as part of her holistic approach to well-being. She believes that by nurturing and nourishing all four levels of our experience as spiritual beings on a human journey, we have a much better chance of accomplishing our mission to evolve and thrive.

For more information visit www.betalksbooks.com

A Note from the Author

Thank you for reading my book!

I felt compelled to reach out as a final note to say how much I appreciate that we are ALL at different stages in our human journey. However, I would argue that 'aborting' our unique mission to explore, expand, and experience can only be made if one is blinded to the awareness, the beauty and the power of who they truly are deep in their core.

I refuse to accept we can't work this one out.

Awareness is everything!

Follow your heart…

Ask important questions,

and above all, sit with your Soul.

Your Divine Soul. That's Who You Truly Are! A Divine Soul in a Sacred Human Body!

'May the Earth
be carpeted with the
Living Flowers
Of our
Loving Actions'

Eliana Regina
www.betalksbooks.com

Also by Eliana Regina

A Book About Us - Celebrating Cultural Diversity
A Book About Us is a collection of four stories by four British children and includes useful tools for personal and social awareness and growth.

Welsh boy Ryan, Sheena from Northern Ireland, Stuart from Scotland, and English young lady Ariana are all in the last year of their respective primary school and are apprehensive as they prepare to transition to 'big school' for their secondary education.

Each with their personal circumstances and life stories to tell, they share a little of their family and cultural backgrounds.

A Book About Us invites young readers across the globe to write a glimpse of their individual stories within the teaching sections found on its pages.

The concept of this book came about originally to educate individuals that Wales is part of the Great Britain landmass along with Northern Ireland, Scotland and England, which is now more commonly known as the United Kingdom, which is, in fact, a corporation. The author, in her travels over the years, found that most people think Wales is in England.

As I worked with the concept, it developed into a social and emotional literacy with focus on personal development.

***

She Speaks Her Truth

She Speaks Her Truth - a mission born from the incredible alchemy that happens when we share our stories, wisdom, and experience of life.

Within the pages of this book, you will find 19 stories written by women from around the world.

Their words, a potential key that will unlock a new perception, knowing, or idea within you as you travel along their journey of life.

It was reading something that sparked a HUGE transformation in my own life. This a simple sentence that changed the trajectory of my life and has now become the driving force and passion behind encouraging women to speak their truth and to share their wisdom; because you never know who is reading, and you never know what magic the words will unlock and the new path that could open for that person.

Enjoy the magical direction this book is about to take you.

Listen to your body as you read.

Allow yourself time to reflect upon the words you read.

She speaks her truth so that you can live yours.

***

The Everyday Girls Guide to Living in Truth, Self-Love, and Acceptance

The Everyday Girls Guide to Living in Truth, Self-Love and Acceptance is the perfect resource of understanding, compassion, and support for teen girls as they navigate this exciting and sometimes daunting chapter of their life, including guidance and wisdom from 19 incredible teen girl mentors from around the world.

This book is brought to you by She Speaks Media, a platform dedicated to creating resources that spark transformation in women and teen girls around the world.

Divine Soul, Sacred Body

Heart Wisdom for the Soul

Be Talks Books is the intellectual property of an amalgamation of forty-two years of professional life that incorporated two careers, first as a Linguist, then as a Counsellor. The founder of Be Talks Books, Eliana Regina, is now investing her time, efforts, and expertise pursuing her third career as an Indie Author. Writing self-awareness and emotional literacy content is what Eliana considers her calling - her life's purpose. Eliana knows at a deep level that her life is not about her but about what she chooses to do with it.

The content of Be Talks Books aims to inform, inspire, educate, and empower individuals who are ready to embark on the quest of discovering who and what they truly are and claim their power back. **Divine Soul, Sacred Body: From Suicide to Sovereignty** is the first book published by Be Talks Books, and the author is working on **Creative Mind, Empowering Emotions: From Awareness to Embodiment**, the sequel to this volume.

Future projects will include Courses, Journals and Workbooks.

Already available is Eliana's signature therapeutic approach, Biogratherapy™, which is an invitation to her readers to write their memoirs with their unique stories and messages to tell in a therapeutic context, guided by Eliana's expertise and metamorphosed as a book you can leave as a legacy to family, friends and the world. Validating our own personal journeys is not only cathartic and healing but also a beautiful and needed way for us to acknowledge one another and connect in a meaningful way.

For more information, email Eliana at eliana@betalksbooks.com

www.betalksbooks.com

Glossary

Innerstand: Knowing that reality arises in language, I have replaced the word 'understand' with innerstand purely from the perspective that I stand in my own inner perception and not 'under' anybody else's. Everything is a frequency that emits a certain vibration, and language in all its expressions, being the source of manifestation, needs special attention. Many words in the English (and other) language(s) are disempowering. I invite the reader to start paying close attention to the words and phrases you have learned to adopt in your daily life.

Solutionary: A new concept has been created in the Visionary and Soul Entrepreneurial circles I am a part of. Humanity needs solutions, so 'solutionaries' are being birthed to help us resolve the many problems we face in our human journey.

Lifeship: Our bodies are the vessels to carry and navigate life with, so whether this word already existed or not, it came through for me while writing this manuscript.

Divine Soul, Sacred Body

References & Links

Bridgend suicide incidents. (2023, January 16). In Wikipedia. https://en.wikipedia.org/wiki/Bridgend_suicide_incidents

Bridgend suicides and Werther effect article
https://www.vanityfair.com/culture/2009/02/wales-suicides200902

Christopher August - Breathwork Alchemist
https://www.christopheraugust.co

Three parts of the cephalic brain
https://www.google.com/search?client=safari&rls=en&q=the+three+brains+joe+dispenza&ie=UTF-8&oe=UTF-8#fpstate=ive&vld=cid:c0529762,vid:8l2nvTv9_Xw

https://www.youtube.com/watch?v=Tq0G6G0jWSI&t=35s
(Saramatu/ Larissa Beattie - Australian)

The three brains in the body:
https://www.thesanghahouse.co.uk/your-three-brains-how-your-head-heart-and-gut-work-together-for-a-better-you

Printed in Great Britain
by Amazon

32796547R00116